YELLOWSTONE

YELLOWSTONE

150 YEARS AS AMERICA'S GREATEST NATIONAL PARK

LEW FREEDMAN

Skyhorse Publishing

Skyhorse Publishing books may be purchased in bulk at special discounts for sales promotion, corporate gifts, fund-raising, or educational purposes. Special editions can also be created to specifications. For details, contact the Special Sales Department, Skyhorse Publishing, 307 West 36th Street, 11th Floor, New York, NY 10018 or info@skyhorsepublishing.com.

Skyhorse® and Skyhorse Publishing® are registered trademarks of Skyhorse Publishing, Inc.®, a Delaware corporation.

Visit our website at www.skyhorsepublishing.com.

10 9 8 7 6 5 4 3 2 1

Library of Congress Cataloging-in-Publication Data is available on file.

Cover design by Kai Texel
Cover photo credits: Getty Images, author images

All photos in this book are by the author unless otherwise notated.

Print ISBN: 978-1-5107-7353-0
Ebook ISBN: 978-1-5107-7354-7

Printed in China

Bison inhabit Yellowstone National Park by the thousands.

Contents

Seeing a grizzly bear in Yellowstone is always a thrill for visitors.

Preface

My first trip to Yellowstone National Park occurred in 2002. It was the year after 9/11, the year after Americans were shocked by the terrorist attacks on the World Trade Center and the Pentagon and by the hijacked plane brought down in Pennsylvania by brave passengers.

After this shaken-to-the-core assault on America, there was a hesitancy to travel to foreign countries, and many Americans chose the staycation option the next summer. When it came to taking a vacation within the borders of the United States, millions of citizens elected to visit Yellowstone, the jewel of the National Parks System and for many a second-generation destination. Their parents had packed up the car and driven them to Wyoming and Montana when they were children, and they decided a repeat for their own children was worthwhile.

At the time I was the outdoors writer for the *Chicago Tribune*, and I joined this migration to remind the Chicago-area readership about the wonders of Yellowstone. I was a first-timer, and it was wonderful, spellbinding, educational, and plain impressive.

Far from the towering, big-city skyscrapers, one was instead surrounded by towering mountains, dense forests, lodgepole pines, spruce and aspen trees, herds of bison crossing the road when least expected—plus bears, elk, deer, and wolves.

The wolves. A phased reintroduction of gray wolves had begun in 1995 and was a source of controversy that continues today. Wolves were shyer than bison and did not like showing themselves near people, so heavy-duty binoculars or super-bazooka camera lenses were the recommended best bets for actually seeing them. Wolves were (and are) despised by many ranchers who believe the animals were put on the planet to kill their cattle. But they are adored by tourists. At the time, the park's chief wolf biologist, Douglas W. Smith, who is still involved with monitoring the packs, said, "It's almost a tidal wave of popularity."

Forget the Loop of downtown Chicago; along with a *Tribune* staff photographer, I drove Grand Loop Road inside the park, pausing at famous sights to chat with visitors, all of whom were soaking up the wilderness experience and the comparative peace removed from traffic jams and noise, the threat of crime, and hustle and bustle congestion.

Seeking solace from the horrifying recent terrorism, Americans returned to their roots of nature. While the country was dipping into a recession in 2002, attendance at Yellowstone was increasing. With its 2.2 million acres, there is a lot of Yellowstone to digest, and it is not difficult to get lost in the grand park in the sense of removing oneself from the larger world to commune with the birds and the trees.

Old Faithful, the geyser, still adhering to its inner clock, erupted on schedule, shooting steam one hundred feet into the air. It never got old, especially for those who had only read about the famous landmark and never seen it spew steam skyward in person.

"It was thrilling," said a grandfather from a Chicago suburb I accosted for his impression after Old Faithful blew its top.

It said something about Americans' souls that in times of a disturbance in the Force, when they were agitated by the world at large, Yellowstone came to mind as a place that would offer a soothing respite. And not only Yellowstone, but the entire National Parks System. An increase in attendance was catalogued across the country, at parks and wildlife refuges and national monuments. They seemed to represent simplicity in a complex time, a source of escape, a reinforcement of what is good about America.

This was true except for at the national park sites near New York City and Washington, DC. People stayed away from the communities that experienced tragedy and their nearby sites. Attendance was way down at the Statue of Liberty in New York and the Lincoln Memorial in Washington. Wounds and memories were too fresh there.

A park ranger told me many visitors chose Yellowstone as a destination "for reflection." She said National Park Service (NPS) personnel did believe there was a link between the terrorism of 2001 and the jump in attendance of 2002.

An old friend who had been a prominent ranger near Denali National Park in Alaska became one of the chief district rangers in Yellowstone near the end of his career. He was very much struck by "the volume of emotions [those iconic parks] evoke." The powerful effect was a reaction to everything from the landscape to the wildlife to what Yellowstone symbolizes for the "benefit and enjoyment of the people." Those words were written into Yellowstone's charter when it became the world's first national park in 1872, and they have always served as an abiding principle.

When living in Alaska, I became used to wildlife mingling with people, from moose resting in the yard or crossing the street in traffic, to black bears popping up unannounced. In Yellowstone, the most frequent likely sighting is of a gigantic bison weighing twelve hundred pounds or more. The bison, more commonly called buffalo in conversation, go where they please. They are often seen strutting down the middle of park roads at the pace of their choice. The speed limit may be posted at forty-five miles per hour for vehicles, but a regularly used phrase to describe a lack of movement on the road is "a bison jam." No red lights slowed traffic, only a bison that felt like stopping, blocking lanes in both directions, and bringing along forty or fifty of his closest friends.

The benefit is this is exactly what visitors have come to see up close. The drawback is, hopefully, those visitors aren't in much of a hurry.

Even now, after myriad advance alerts and incidents, individuals amazingly do not heed warnings to stay at least twenty-five yards from bison and seem oblivious to the great danger of taking up-close bison selfies. Rick Wallen, the longtime park bison specialist, said people must be reminded Yellowstone is not a zoo. That is a credo of Yellowstone Park personnel.

Naive visitors wish to see animals fed, perhaps something they saw on a television nature show. Not in Yellowstone. Nature is natural, and marching orders are to leave the animals be. The former Alaska-turned-Yellowstone ranger admitted to a double-take when once asked, "When do you bring the wildlife in for the night?"

Where to go first? Where to go next? The charms of Yellowstone are many, and seduce one into long pauses. The Upper Falls and the Lower Falls of the Yellowstone River are inviting, and it is difficult to leave the waterfalls behind. Likewise Fountain Geyser. Nathaniel P. Langford, the first superintendent of Yellowstone, was appointed after it became a park in 1872; he was also a member of a preliminary exploration party, and those expedition travelers were Yellowstone virgins as they approached sights on horseback.

"These wonders are so different from anything we have ever seen," Langford wrote, adding, "from the moment they began to appear until we left them has been one of intense surprise and of incredulity."

It was the same way for me, and the park continues to provide startling first impressions—and renewed impressions—for the millions who tour Yellowstone each year.

LEW FREEDMAN
March 2022

Introduction

Yellowstone National Park was anointed with its status as the nation's first national park, as well as the world's, in 1872, a symbol of groundbreaking and wise American policy providing a leading example for other countries at a time when the United States' mindset was more focused on Manifest Destiny.

It was one of the pioneering examples, just as Yosemite had been, of mankind taking a step back from aggressive, blind development with a first glance toward long-term preservation for future generations. There seemed to be an awakening to the riches of landscape the United States possessed and the dawning of an awareness that if not careful, a reckless human presence could ruin it all. This was very much a political process, as well as a bold departure in thinking that land, scenery, and wildlife could be valuable for their own sakes, not merely for the cash value of harvesting crops or minerals.

Through its growing pains, management challenges, natural evolution, and humans' own attempts to diminish what was initially wrought through natural creation and then through government lawmaking, Yellowstone became the signature of a vast National Park System.

When famed documentary maker Ken Burns turned his attention to the parks, the theme of the film was "America's best idea." The camera capturing the beauty set aside for long-term protection served as a reminder of the premise announced when Yellowstone was established: the goal was to preserve things the way they were for the enjoyment and appreciation of grandchildren and great-grandchildren yet unborn. *Don't sell out the future.*

Millions upon millions of Americans, and enchanted tourists from around the globe, have visited Yellowstone to see why it has been viewed as the crown jewel of the park system for the last century and a half. Of course, Yellowstone land was there long before the US government drew boundaries around it to delineate a park. The trees, lakes, thermal features, rivers, canyons, and mountains were formed eons ago and they sit atop the Yellowstone Caldera, a dormant volcano.

Periodically, the ground shifts and shakes, setting off measurable earthquake tremors, though much milder than what has been projected to come someday. There are paranoid long-distance Richter-scale followers who telephone the NPS offices inside Yellowstone any time they hear of a quake. This sets off a chain reaction of pacification from the National Park Service, which must announce that the Yellowstone Caldera is not about to blow its top and annihilate a vast area. It is commonly said the last truly major seismic activity in Yellowstone took place six hundred thousand years ago, and that if the Caldera ever becomes a menace, people will have months or years of advance warning.

Thus the geologic history of Yellowstone is far more ancient than the comparatively short span of one hundred fifty years under which the park land has been under the supervision of the United States government.

Historians believe that for perhaps eleven thousand years Native Americans of the region freely traversed this land, hunting, fishing, traveling, and appreciating the wealth of food supplies. The Native Americans did not install permanent settlements, establish villages, or make property claims the way European men would have by staking a flag on fresh territory.

Nez Percé and Shoshone tribes were prominent in the area, and the early fur traders who encountered these souls were told fabulous stories about the bounty of wildlife, as well as steaming earth they had no frame of reference for. Western

On a rare occasion people can see elk battling for supremacy during the rutting season, as these two are at Mammoth Hot Springs.

explorers could not envision the boiling springs described.

The Lewis and Clark Expedition, sent west by President Thomas Jefferson to explore unmapped lands in the Rocky Mountains and to check out some of the lands the United States acquired from France with the Louisiana Purchase, thoroughly investigated everywhere except for the Yellowstone area during its three years on the road. While consorting with the Native Americans of the area in present-day Montana, Meriwether Lewis, William Clark, and their Corps of Discovery did hear stories about Yellowstone, and did overlap slightly with Yellowstone territory, but they did not alter their planned course for intensive inspection.

The Yellowstone River is a tributary of the Missouri. The Native Americans of the region referred to the large, swiftly flowing, 692-mile-long river, with its headwaters contained in what became the park, as the "Yellow Rock River" in the Hidatsa language. That morphed into Yellowstone, as the name of the river and the park. The name stuck for good, and Yellowstone became one of the most famous places in the country.

Popular enough to attract nearly 4.9 million visitors in a year, Yellowstone remains wild enough to require a guarded approach in keeping safe from wildlife. The foolish or reckless sometimes find themselves in dire straits after dangerously treading on the home ground of large animals with no inhibitions and with a determination to protect their young as well as their personal space. Somehow, the occasional visitor disregards the warning memos the National Park Service hands out to people at entrance gates to make sure they comprehend the rules of the park.

Yellowstone has passed through many stages, from the geological formation era of millions of years ago, to what would have to be characterized as a modern era of management shakily begun in 1872, up to the present day. Current park superintendent Cameron "Cam" Sholly said only in the last fifty years or so has an enlightened management program really focused on all-around preservation.

For many people, Yellowstone represents their favorite place on earth, the most beautiful paradise on the planet, a place somehow accessible yet mostly unspoiled, in accordance with its original pledge to future generations.

Yes, there are admission fees and there are rules to be followed, but Yellowstone and the other national parks, preserves, refuges, and monuments are locations held in trust "for the People," for all of us, managed by the federal government with the goal of forever being available to the people.

To many, Yellowstone is the flagship symbol of that entire system, because it is so otherworldly compared to many Americans' home areas, especially the big cities, where there are no grizzly bears, nor trout streams, nor dense forests.

The People come for a once-in-a-lifetime trip, but many come back again and again, not wanting their trip to end.

The scenery of Yellowstone lured early explorers to investigate what was in the region. A multitude of small waterfalls are sprinkled around the park.

CHAPTER 1

Yellowstone Before It Was a Park

"Occupation: Frontiersman" was one simple term describing the mountain men who roamed the western United States in the earliest days of the country. They were hardy men who hunted and trapped and lived off the land in the harsh conditions winter delivered to the Rocky Mountains.

They were also the first White Americans to see Yellowstone National Park, their views supplementing Native American tales of monstrously sized grizzly bears, millions of bison, and vast empty spaces of raw land.

Mountain men made their living in a hard way, and when they gathered for a rendezvous they were known to tell stories of challenges conquered alone in difficult conditions. No one was administrating lie-detector tests when tales were swapped at these festivals. So they earned a reputation as men for whom lying was a pastime, for whom exaggerating came naturally, for whom a yarn might well be embellished to the edge of credulity, if not beyond the boundary of believability.

For that reason, what those bold mountain men related seeing in Yellowstone country often remained within a tight circle of listeners. It was one thing to exaggerate among compadres, another to have your word passed on to polite society. It was often said mountain men experienced remarkable things that were true but did not wish to risk being accused of being liars.

As if it did not accomplish enough during its arduous journey, the Lewis and Clark Expedition might have become explorers of the Yellowstone region as well if they had time for a little detour. But they pushed forward on their set path, skirting the edges.

However, unlike Meriwether Lewis, William Clark, and most of their retinue, who were pleased to return to their homes when the expedition concluded in 1806, John Colter requested permission to stay behind in the wild. Colter is considered the first White American to enter the Yellowstone territory and explore within the region, essentially following up on some of the stories told to the expedition by Native Americans.

Recordkeeping was sketchier in Colter's time, especially if one was not born in a city or didn't have a Bible handy within a family for a birthdate to be marked down. It is believed Colter was born between 1770 and 1775 in the Colony of Virginia. His forebears in North America seem to trace to 1700 after emigrating from Ireland. The American Revolutionary War broke out at roughly the same time as his birth, and by the time Colter approached adulthood there was a United States.

Colter's family moved to Kentucky, and in those days that area was the West. This is where Daniel Boone made his initial mark, and a young man such as Colter could hone hunting skills and logically aspire to become a mountain man. The opportunity to join Lewis and Clark was appealing, and on the expedition Colter was paid five dollars a day as he distinguished himself as an adept hunter providing meat for the travelers.

Increasingly, Lewis and Clark entrusted Colter with more important missions, and when he moved through rough areas on assignment he encountered local Nez Percé tribal members and befriended them. As the Corps of Discovery turned back east, it came upon two trappers, and Colter received permission to split from Lewis and Clark two months ahead of schedule to become their guide.

Colter became a trapper, mostly seeking

beaver, with his new partners. By 1807, he and his backwoods companions were regulars in future Montana and Wyoming, men who rode, trapped, and hunted the Yellowstone area.

Traversing these unnamed, unmapped areas, Colter and the others also explored areas that later acquired well-known names: Grand Teton National Park, Jackson Hole (Jackson, Wyoming), the Wind River area, and Idaho.

Colter used Fort Raymond, Montana, as a base. A trading post built by fur trader Manuel Lisa, it served as a gathering spot. There Colter reported seeing fantastic hot spots, pools of bubbling water now known as thermal features. No one knew what he was talking about, and he was considered a fabricator, a creator of tall tales. This was the mountain man's lot. Colter insisted what he saw was real. Beyond that he encountered a river, which he called "Stinking Water," because it smelled awfully foul. Its name was later changed to the Shoshone River, and the smell Colter sniffed was sulfur.

The more Colter talked, the more he was disbelieved. Later, all that he said was confirmed as true, and this region came to be called "Colter's Hell."

While not as gifted a cartographer as Amerigo Vespucci or Ferdinand Magellan, Colter's shaky hand produced a map of the route he thought he traveled and which later became Wyoming. No one has ever been 100 percent sure of Colter's precise course, though.

Up to that point, despite being dismissed as a man who wielded a false tongue, Colter had been fairly lucky. He had done well in establishing himself as a good trapper. Then, in 1808, he was attacked by Native Americans and wounded by an arrow. A year later, he was captured, robbed, stripped, and told to get out of the country by members of another tribe. He had to run for it and fight for his life.

Eventually, Colter gave up the mountains and settled, with a new wife, in St. Louis. In 1810, he met with William Clark and told him of the adventures he experienced after the men went their separate ways.

The date of Colter's death is not clear. Two different dates, May 7, 1812, and November 22, 1813, are given. An historical marker in Stuarts Draft, Virginia, honors his memory. It refers to him as being born "about 1775" and credits him as follows: "Colter traversed the area now comprising Yellowstone National Park and discovered several passes through the Rocky Mountains suitable for wagon trains."

Although surely John Colter never received apologies from his doubters, he was not lying about the glories he saw in the Yellowstone area. Those thermal features were quite real; the cauldrons of two-hundred-degree water and gushing, cloud-like steam blowing into the air may not have been part of his contemporaries' frames of reference, but they were very genuine phenomena.

Yellowstone contains a variety of hot spots, hot springs, mud pots, and fumaroles. They erupt, sputter, bubble, steam, and are widely distributed across the park's nearly 3,500 square miles. It has been estimated there are about ten thousand thermal features inside the Yellowstone National Park, most situated within geyser basins.

The park has nine geyser basin areas, and within their separate regions there are hundreds of geysers. What is called the Upper Geyser Basin alone has 410 geysers, the Lower Geyser Basin 283, Norris Geyser Basin 193, Shoshone Geyser Basin 107, and West Thumb Geyser Basin 84.

Scientists have calculated that nearly 1,300 geysers have erupted at some point, and 465 erupt in an average year. It is very dangerous, and strictly forbidden, for visitors to trek near the geysers. Humans risk serious injury or death from burns if they are careless, or they may damage the fragile surrounding ground in plodding approaches.

Scientists indicate about half the world's geysers are located in Yellowstone National Park; other hot spots for geyser activity are located in Iceland, Russia, Chile, and New Zealand. Chile has more geysers than any other nation in the Southern Hemisphere. New Zealand has had some of its geysers destroyed. Iceland has fewer than thirty geysers, but a very high percentage of active ones. Russia's Valley of Geysers on the Kamchatka Peninsula has the second largest concentration of geysers after Yellowstone, with two hundred.

Some thermal features emit almost continuous steam. Some erupt regularly. Some practically never erupt. Some are located very close to public access routes and can easily be seen erupting, while others are deep in the backcountry and are never seen erupting except possibly by hikers and campers, or National Park Service personnel on patrol.

The most famous thermal feature in Yellowstone National Park, one of its highlight attractions, is Old Faithful. The geyser was named because it erupts on a regular time schedule. It is also easily viewed by crowds congregating in a boardwalk area.

Old Faithful has stuck to a train-like schedule for centuries, though it has varied a little over time. During the summer of 2020, Old Faithful erupted roughly every one-and-a-half hours for a duration of four minutes. There is a plus or minus factor predicted within the timetable of around ten minutes each way, earlier or later. Mostly, Old Faithful has erupted every forty-four minutes to two hours since 2000.

The boiling water is thrust skyward during the eruption, at a height that is somewhat predictable. The water will fly skyward at least one hundred feet and sometimes may approach two hundred feet in the air. Witnesses gasp in awe in response.

Although the temperature of water exploding through a vent has been estimated at 204 degrees Fahrenheit, once the water is free of the cone it quickly begins to cool and is no longer of a fiery nature by the time it strikes the ground.

Fumaroles are steam vents considered to be the hottest of the hot spots within Yellowstone. They are dryer than other spots, and they throw up steam before the release reaches the surface.

Hot springs give off heated water. The most famous hot spring is the Grand Prismatic Spring; it is located in Midway Geyser Basin and is the third largest hot spring in the world. It's known for the spectacular colored water it shows off, and the feature sometimes appears red, orange, yellow, blue, and green.

Mud pots are more acidic, thus producing sulfur content that causes the areas such as that of Mud Volcano and Fountain Paint Pot to emit a pungent aroma. Rock decays into clay in these areas, and youngsters are known to ask their parents "What's that smell?" while viewing the mud pots.

The travertine terraces at Mammoth Hot Springs have their own look. The rock-like cliffs are made of limestone, and the coloration appears white instead of what most visitors would expect when looking at a rock feature. Many people confuse them with ice formations, but they retain their unique look in warm temperatures.

Old Faithful is the most famous thermal feature in Yellowstone, and the geyser erupts on a semi-regular schedule, to the delight of tourists, every hour or so.

Such sights as the mud volcano, where sloppy stuff gurgled out of the ground, surprised Yellowstone's first explorers, who had no idea what might appear around the next bend.

The eye-catching travertine terraces at Mammoth Hot Springs resemble ice formations.

One of Colter's trapping partners, with whom he shared many dangers, was Daniel T. Potts. Colter may have been illiterate, but Potts was not. Potts wrote a letter to his brother dated July 8, 1827, in what has been called the first written description of Yellowstone's geysers. In part it reads:

"On the south borders of this lake [Yellowstone Lake] is a number of hot and boiling springs—some of water and others of the most beautiful fine clay. . . . [The spring] throws its particles to the immense height of from twenty to thirty feet in height. The clay is white and of a pink. . . . There is also a number of places where the pure sulfur is sent forth in abundance."

While many did not believe Colter's words, some were intrigued. A fellow named W. A. Ferris, a clerk for the American Fur Company, listened and decided he wished to see such strange phenomena himself.

Ferris was present at a rendezvous in 1833, at what became Daniel, Wyoming, and the storytelling caught his fancy. A year later he was motivated to journey to an area "that remarkable boiling springs had been discovered, on the sources of the Madison [River] by a party of trappers in their spring hunt; of which the accounts they gave were so very astonishing that I determined to examine them myself." Ferris said he collected some twenty accounts of visitors to these hot springs before seeing them for himself.

Ferris wrote of reaching his destination at night, but then waking the next day surrounded by steam emanating from underground boiling areas. "When I arose in the morning," he said, "clouds of vapor seemed like a dense fog to overhang the springs, from which frequent reports or explosions of different loudness, constantly assailed our ears."

The uniqueness of such sights exceeded in grandeur the descriptions delivered by other trappers by such a great amount that Ferris's reaction was, "The half was not told me." He also quickly made the acquaintance of the smell of sulfur and noted how it assaulted his nose.

"From the surface of a rocky plain or table," Ferris reported, "burst forth columns of water, of various dimensions, projected high in the air, accompanied by loud explosions, and sulfurous vapors, which were highly disagreeable to the smell."

Ferris allowed that the plumes were "wonderful fountains" erupting at intervals of about two hours. Almost like a child, he was drawn to the water, but he learned quite quickly if he reached his hand out, the water was too hot to the touch. "The Indians who were with me were quite appalled," Ferris wrote of men (who had clearly been there before and knew what they were doing), "and could not by any means be induced to approach them."

It did not take very long for those who encountered hot springs in the Yellowstone region to adopt such a common-sense outlook. High temperatures aside, the Native Americans, said Ferris, viewed the springs as being of supernatural origin that had been created by "the Evil Spirit."

The good old "super volcano," as the underground activity is often referred to today, a percolating mass of steam and hot water that everyone thinks will blow up and wipe Yellowstone off the map, is more often the subject of jokes because few think the cataclysm will take place while they are standing on top of it.

National Geographic seems forever to be peering over the shoulders of the oblivious and worrywarts alike. In articles, the publication has discussed the prospect of a big bang while at other times wondering if there is some way to harness and make good use of all that energy.

In 2018, the magazine reported that "a massive magma chamber feeds this super volcano and an eruption would pack enough power to expel more than a thousand cubic kilometers of rock and ash at once. That would blanket most of the continental United States in debris and potentially plunge Earth into a volcanic winter."

That was a pessimistic outlook, to say the least. The same report mentioned big bang believers think a response might be to drill a series of wells and while "pumping cold water down into the hot rock" prevent any such major problem. Five gigawatts of electricity could be obtained for energy, turning the super volcano into a power plant.

This is an idea, but not close to happening. Since the super volcano might not erupt for a thousand or more years, there is no pressing deadline to test out this option.

The thermal features may have won the derisive name of "Colter's Hell" from John Colter's fellow mountain men, but Jim Bridger, who had a widespread reputation as one of those intrepid wilderness wanderers a little bit later, was not offended by such characterizations. Bridger was born in 1804 and lived until 1881, mostly making his living in the fur trade. Orphaned young, he was illiterate but a genius at survival in the wild, and when he saw those same thermal features he was at no loss for words, saying Yellowstone was "the place where Hell bubbled up."

Using hell as a comparison point for Yellowstone's thermal features seems dramatic for what is now embraced as a tourist attraction, but the thermal features were eye-catching and had not been explained to a less scientifically oriented populace. The thermal features are only hell now for those who take missteps and fall in, or dare to see if it makes sense to bathe in them (it does not), or for those who escape only with fines from the National Park Service from traversing the areas.

While Old Faithful may be the biggest draw because of its enduring fame and reliability, someone touring the park will run across many different geyser basins, spot steam from afar in many regions of the park, and may, out of sheer luck, rather than setting their watch based on a prediction, come across an eruption of breathtaking proportion.

One of those less predictable but well-known geysers in Yellowstone is Steamboat Geyser. Steamboat is located in the Norris Geyser Basin, and Yellowstone officials refer to it as the world's largest active geyser. When it goes off it can spew water, steam, and rock three hundred feet into the air. Only a geyser in New Zealand has hurled such debris higher, but it has not done so in over one hundred years.

When Steamboat blows, it sends sheets of water into the air, as if emulating a pounding rainstorm. Rock and sand can land on automobile windshields and ding cars, if any are nearby. Although Steamboat's eruptions may last much longer (up to forty minutes) and are more powerful than Old Faithful's (sometimes knocking down grown trees), it does not operate on a strict schedule, but more on its own whim.

Steamboat has been more active in recent years, but has gone through decades-long periods with no eruptions whatsoever, so it does not pay for tourists to schedule vacations around a stop there.

It is not believed Steamboat erupted at all between 1911 and 1961 and not at all between 2014 and 2018, when, it might be said, it began picking up steam. Since 2018, there have been steady, though irregular eruptions, with forty-eight eruptions in 2019 alone. The pace remained steady in 2020. It is uncertain, but this could be the heyday of Steamboat eruptions.

Perhaps some of its cachet is due to the catchy name, but Old Faithful has long been a key destination inside Yellowstone. It is the geyser most American and foreign visitors are familiar with and most want to see. There is even bleacher seating laid out in a slight arc facing the geyser for the crowds that accumulate. At any given summer eruption, there may be one thousand witnesses to the semi-scheduled eruptions.

The Old Faithful Inn, constructed in 1904, is just a few steps from the geyser and is also a signature building of Yellowstone. On scorching hot days, or those that are freezing cold, visitors who may have just missed an eruption can enter a gift shop, eat a meal, or rest in the huge log structure while waiting for the next one.

Yellowstone is basically about scenery and

wildlife, but the Old Faithful Inn holds a special place in the minds of park fans and supporters. Author John Clayton says tourists may feel sheepish about hanging out in a building inside Yellowstone, instead of spending all their time doing something worthwhile outdoors. But Clayton wrote they should not feel such guilt and instead appreciate the building's history in the park.

"This remarkable building influenced many subsequent prominent structures in national and state parks. And it helped change people's expectations of park experiences—how we want buildings to relate to the natural environment and how we want other tourists to relate to us."

The hotel is one of the few log hotels still in business in the United States, and it houses a fireplace containing 450 metric tons of stone. The Inn itself was named a National Historic Landmark in 1987. Appropriately, from the upstairs porch, a visitor can watch an Old Faithful eruption, though the hotel can't handle as many viewers who wish to watch at a given time.

That's why the bleachers exist, to give the tourists an unobstructed photographic view of the geyser.

Mountains dot the landscape in Yellowstone, some reaching eleven thousand-plus feet tall.

CHAPTER 2

John Muir and Yosemite, Jim Bridger and Yellowstone

One of John Muir's nicknames is "Father of the National Parks." The most famous naturalist of his time, and perhaps of all time, Muir was essentially the father of conservation.

If the United States government had been more ready, more far-seeing, Yosemite, not Yellowstone, would have been the world's first national park. As a result of the urgings and lobbying of Muir, Yosemite was the first such place in the country set aside as a park worthy of being preserved. However, the concept of going national had not quite taken hold yet. When President Abraham Lincoln signed the Yosemite Grant in 1864, no one knew how to handle this park's administration, so it was turned over to California and became a state park.

There was much resistance to the idea of making land off limits to business interests, and verbal battles and political maneuvering followed. Muir may have believed he had won the war when Yosemite received its presidential recognition, but that was not the case. It was not until 1890, when an expanded Yosemite in the Sierra Nevada mountains became a national park some eighteen years after Yellowstone was established.

Muir, who lived from 1838 to 1914, was a pioneer with vision. He was unselfish in the sense that much of his life's work was aimed at a future he would never see. A founder of the Sierra Club, which currently has about 2.4 million members, Muir was an indefatigable fighter for preservation.

Muir hiked and explored backcountry regions for years and energetically wrote about what he saw, how it affected him, and how he believed wilderness could positively affect men's souls and well-being. When Muir wasn't walking, he was writing down his impressions formed while walking, in letters to friends or government officials in high places, in hundreds of magazine articles and essays, and in books still read today.

Famously, Muir took a camping trip in Yosemite in 1903 with then-president Theodore Roosevelt, a private and personal visit considered extremely influential. Roosevelt was a founder of the Boone and Crockett Club and instituted the National Wildlife Refuge System, a few of his outdoors-related achievements that still resonate today.

Yosemite was Muir's pet project and his personal symbol of what mattered about the country as the world encroached, developed, and threatened to demolish the territory that made the United States special. Without John Muir and the advance work on Yosemite, it is questionable whether there would have been a Yellowstone National Park in 1872.

To Muir, Yosemite was a spiritual place, difficult to describe in words, but once experienced irresistible to the heart and mind. "It is easier to feel than to realize, or in any way explain, Yosemite grandeur," Muir said. "The magnitudes of the rocks and trees and streams are so delicately harmonized, they are mostly hidden."

That magical image worked on Roosevelt in an expansive sense, as applied to other patches of America.

"The coniferous forests of Yosemite Park, and of the Sierra in general, surpass all others of their kind in America, or indeed the world," Muir also noted, "not only in the size and beauty of the trees, but in the number of species assembled together, and the grandeur of the mountains they are growing on."

It is obvious Muir's mind was predisposed to appreciate outdoor marvels. He was infuriated to a fighting degree whenever he learned many despoilers of the land were more interested in chopping down trees, poaching wildlife, and profiting from these American landscapes in Yosemite, Yellowstone, and elsewhere, with no thought given to what would remain behind for their grandchildren. These battles were not quickly dispensed, but long, drawn-out litigations and, more importantly, the spreading establishment of mindsets.

What Yosemite and Yellowstone stood for was a new argument taking shape in the American psyche: there was wilderness worth saving for wilderness's sake, and that conservation for those yet unborn was important. Forward-thinking people did not want to be culpable to future generations, blamed for the ruination of and elimination of what America once had and was. It is a battle that continues on some levels well into the twenty-first century.

John Muir's commitment to Yosemite led to the nation's commitment to Yellowstone. That was after people got past the notion that John Colter and other mountain men spoke about things that indeed were quite real and were not horrors, but riches.

The mountain men did not navigate by GPS but rode on horseback through isolated regions (regions, of course, previously explored by Native Americans). These were trappers and hunters who made a living trading furs with the locals and by dealing the furs to traders who shipped them east. Yet they did not ship their stories east for some time.

In their regular travels, these rugged men, who grew great beards and dressed themselves in the same skins as the animals they hunted, followed a route called the Bannock Trail. It stretched from what became the state of Idaho across what became the state of Wyoming while cutting through Yellowstone.

These men were using the trail, named after the Bannock tribe, for transportation, not with exploration on their minds. The trail was known as early as 1837 and was in use for the next forty years. Yellowstone was characterized by very rough terrain, and the nearby Rocky Mountains pointed skyward at more than fourteen thousand feet in Colorado.

Many years before Yellowstone acquired a following, settlers were traveling west, on the Oregon Trail as early as 1842 and for the California Gold Rush in 1848. These people were determined to find farm land to raise families or to strike it rich in the gold fields. They were not so interested in the pristine and unique Yellowstone land that lay in between.

In 1860, although the nation was about to be very much preoccupied by the devastating and bloody Civil War, an expedition was mounted to investigate some of the stories the mountain men were spreading. Captain William F. Raynolds was a military officer in charge of the group, which was guided by scout Jim Bridger.

Originally, Raynolds was not a believer in Bridger's reports. He scoffed at the setting of the rendezvous, where no doubt these vacationing men had been under the influence of generous amounts of liquor. Raynolds thought it likely these fellows, Bridger included, "should beguile the monotony of camp life by spinning yarns in which each tried to excel all others, and which were repeated so often and insisted upon so strenuously that the narrators came to believe them most religiously."

Another officer, a captain named Eugene F. Ware, based at Fort Laramie, commented on Bridger's convincing speaking demeanor in 1864. "Major Bridger was a regular old Roman in actions and appearances," Ware reported, "and he told stories in such a solemn and firm, convincing way that a person would be likely to believe him." Ware said Bridger had a tendency to add bluster to his stories with "statements which were ludicrous, sometimes greatly exaggerated and sometimes imaginary." Not about Yellowstone, though. Reality was juicy enough.

Scenic wonders such as the Grand Canyon of the Yellowstone waterfall were so marvelous that reports from mountain man Jim Bridger and conservationist John Muir were selling points endorsing "forever" preservation of the park.

Perhaps unusual in Ware's experience of mingling with other frontiersmen, he said Bridger was not an "egotistic liar" who boasted in stories of his own achievements and bravery, but "always had reference to some outdoor matter or circumstance."

Such as a mysterious geyser that would spout one hundred feet into the air. The geyser stuff checked out. Bridger's fanciful discussions of Yellowstone featuring petrified forests, populated by petrified birds singing petrified songs, not so much.

As an individual, the unschooled Bridger earned a reputation as a man of great stamina who worked hard in the wilderness and had a knack for surviving and thriving. He did see it all

in the Yellowstone area during his days of roaming the wild and got to know many of the famed westerners of the period. He was acquainted, to one degree or another, with General George Armstrong Custer, scout Kit Carson, and other mountain men such as Hugh Glass, Joseph Meek, and Jedediah Smith.

Bridger did not write memoirs, but he told tales, and sometimes listeners wrote them down, including some of his impressions about Yellowstone. One of them featured Obsidian Cliff. Obsidian typically occurs in rocks that have broken off and fallen to the ground. Bridger told people the rock glowed in the moonshine, and this was a unique obsidian formation. Humans have retrieved obsidian from the cliff for approximately eleven thousand years; in modern times, in 1996, it was designated a National Historic Landmark.

Well before Raynolds led his trip, Bridger drew a map of the trail he regularly followed, in 1851 on behalf of some French travelers. It included the Grand Canyon of the Yellowstone, Yellowstone Lake, and the headwaters of the Yellowstone River. There were markings for the Gibbon, Madison, and Gallatin rivers.

Not everything he placed was precisely accurate, but when he wasn't teasing people, Bridger essentially knew what he was talking about.

Pierre-Jean De Smet, who was with Bridger in 1851, studied Bridger's work and comments and then added his own observations, taking note of "a mountain of sulfur." This was Mammoth Hot Springs, near the park's north entrance today. Another United States officer, Lieutenant J. W. Gunnison, did not claim Bridger was a supernatural cartographer but someone who made major contributions to understanding the terrain, praising him in a less formal manner than might usually be found in official documents. Gunnison said of Bridger, "He has been very active and traversed the region. . . . His graphic sketches are delightful romances. With a buffalo skin and a piece of charcoal, he will map out any portion of this immense region, and delineate mountains, streams, and the circular valleys called 'holes' with wonderful accuracy."

Raynolds, who was assigned by the US Army Corps of Topographical Engineers to lead the 1860 journey, was told to figure out the best way to travel between the Yellowstone River and South Pass, and to determine if there was a way to connect the Wood River to the Missouri.

That was all well and good, but Bridger, his guide, knew too much about the land and said the aim of the group was faulty. "I told you, you could not go through," Bridger said. "A bird can't fly over that without taking a supply of grub along."

Raynolds tried another route, but the heavy snows of the region, arriving much earlier than the easterner expected, cut him off from the wonders of Yellowstone. He had heard so much and wanted the truth, but Raynolds came away frustrated by his circumstances. "We were compelled to content ourselves with listening to marvelous tales of burning plains, immense lakes, and boiling springs, without being able to verify these wonders," he said.

One relayed comment from Bridger that struck Raynolds, however, was explaining how one boiling spring "is the very counterpart of the geysers of Iceland." Indeed, when more knowledge spread, comparisons were widely made between the geysers of Iceland and the geysers of Yellowstone.

Then the Civil War intervened, with all hands on deck for the Union Army fighting the secession of the South. Raynolds ultimately turned in a map of the journey through Yellowstone, but not for five years. Too many other pressing national concerns took priority.

It was surprising enough that President Lincoln took the time to sign a government document providing special status to Yosemite in 1864 when the Civil War was going strong; a

For those who hadn't seen such a phenomenon with their own eyes, it was difficult to believe that the ground could steam and throw boiling water skyward.

more detailed investigation of Yellowstone would have to come later.

Bridger was married and living on a farm near Kansas City, Missouri, when he died at seventy-seven years old, not a mountain in sight. In later years, demonstrating how much he got around, many things besides the community of about seven hundred people in Montana (located 230 miles from the entrance to Yellowstone National Park) were named after him.

There has been a Fort Bridger in Wyoming, schools and streets named for him in different western states, and, more appropriately, forests and mountains.

There is also an annual Jim Bridger Days festival in Bridger, Montana, each July.

Fountain Paint Pots, one of the many colorful thermal features in Yellowstone.

Even the Lewis and Clark Expedition's Corps of Discovery, sent west by President Thomas Jefferson to see what was out there, was warned about the danger of underestimating the grizzly bear.

CHAPTER 3
Becoming a Park

The world's first national park was created on March 1, 1872, when President Ulysses S. Grant signed a piece of legislation called "The Act of Dedication."

That formally brought Yellowstone National Park into being. Much had occurred since the days of John Colter and the early days of Jim Bridger. Much more would transpire before Yellowstone morphed into the park we know today.

Only gradually, between Captain William Raynolds and Grant's approval, had Yellowstone's properties become somewhat better recognized as fact more than fiction, as genuine, tangible, and unusual wonders more than subjects of fanciful claims. Over time, the contents of the Yellowstone region had transformed from wild to wilderness.

Not everyone who spread the word about Yellowstone experienced enduring fame as did John Muir and Jim Bridger. One of the key supporters and explorers who helped bring forth the message of Yellowstone was Ferdinand V. Hayden, well-known in Yellowstone annals but not a name in the forefront of Americans' memories.

Born in 1829 in Westfield, Massachusetts, Hayden was a nature lover, a doctor, and a geologist. In 1860 he was a member of the Raynolds-Bridger group that had so ached to see and describe the thermal features, but failed. In the end, Hayden would play a critical role in public acceptance of Yellowstone.

The intervention of the Civil War ate up half the decade between Raynolds's trip and the remainder of the 1860s, but by the terminus of those years, others were engaging in exploration attempts to find out more about what lay in the dense forests so difficult to reach in Yellowstone territory.

Hayden was an organizer and leader of explorations determined to investigate the Rocky Mountains, but he always steered slightly wide of Yellowstone in the late 1860s. Although Hayden's final expedition in 1871 was the clincher in terms of convincing Congress to provide support for Yellowstone's establishment as a national park, in some ways he was also scooped.

In 1869, Charles W. Cook, David E. Folsom, and William Peterson, three men from Diamond City, Montana, near Helena, privately funded a truly organized exploration of Yellowstone. Unlike what had transpired in the past when mountain men who had passed through relayed anecdotal tales, two of these men (Cook and Folsom) kept meticulous journals that brought considerable attention to Yellowstone. Basically, they wrote down everything they saw.

Originally, the trio planned to be part of a different expedition, but that group fell apart and the threesome joined together. They set out on September 6, 1869, and for the next five weeks toured the region before returning to Diamond City on October 11.

As the trio set off, they had no delusions of grandeur, nor any sense of grand purpose other than curiosity. Well-wishers ushering them into the wilderness teased them, perhaps couching their nervousness about their health in semi-sarcastic comments.

Were there jokesters in the crowd, or seriously worried supporters? Someone said, "Goodbye boys, look out for your hair" as a warning against being scalped by the Native Americans in the Yellowstone region. Someone else said, "It's the next thing to suicide." Much later, Cook revealed his impression of the mood at the departure spot in Diamond City. "It has assumed proportions of utter insignificance," Cook wrote of the trip, "and of no importance to anybody in the world except the three actors themselves." Yet off they went by horseback, returning with their hair and some vivid descriptions.

The men traveled along the Missouri River, through the Gallatin Valley, to the Yellowstone River, encountered the confluence of the Yellowstone and the Gardner River near present-day Gardiner, Montana, continued to Tower Fall, passed along the Lamar River, and came to the Yellowstone Falls and the Grand Canyon of the Yellowstone, seeing some of the most magnificent waterfalls in America.

They reached the shore of Yellowstone Lake and went on to West Thumb, crossed the Continental Divide, and came to Shoshone Lake. They followed the Firehole River near geysers to the Madison River, coming to the area where West Yellowstone, Montana, now stands. They were gone for thirty-six days.

The diaries kept by Cook and Folsom (perhaps with some input from Peterson) were shared with others, including mapmaker W. W. deLacy, who found their descriptions more detailed than Jim Bridger's old freehand work. Folsom actually went to work for Henry Washburn, the surveyor general of Montana Territory, which was a fortuitous match.

Some of Folsom's friends urged him to give a public talk about Yellowstone and its wonders, but he hesitated, fearful he would be lumped in with the doubted mountain men, especially when it came to discussing those thermal features. One of those friends was Nathaniel P. Langford, who soon enough would have his own life transformed by Yellowstone National Park.

While there may still have been Yellowstone skeptics seated in Folsom's audience of so-called prominent Helena citizens, many others, who recognized his reputation for honesty, believed his report. It also caught the fancy of others who wanted to know more—and see more.

Still, Folsom was correct to worry about overall reaction. He and Cook combined their journals into one volume and submitted it to *The New York Times* for possible publication. Although *The Times* has featured the phrase "All the News That's Fit to Print" as a motto, it failed to print this missive because it could not vouch for its authenticity. Likewise, when the authors' product was read by Scribner's, the book publisher, it was rejected for the same reason. Decades later, the entire combined journals, plus additions of Peterson's own reminiscences, saw print. In some instances these were billed as "reconstructed" diaries.

It is common for explorers who are the first to see, analyze, and discover new geologic features, such as mountains, lakes, and rivers, to name them. Sometimes the expedition members have places named for them, and other times they are named for loved ones. During the Cook–Folsom–Peterson adventure, they took copious notes but did not name anything for anyone. Sometime later, however, mountains were named after Cook (Cook Peak, 9,754 feet) and Folsom (Folsom Peak, 9,334 feet), but not for Peterson.

This minor expedition accomplished a fair amount, particularly as part of a continuum that kept interest in Yellowstone expanding, slowly, if not in booming fashion.

What became known as the Washburn Expedition, or the Washburn–Langford–Doane Expedition of 1870, followed Cook, Folsom, and Peterson. Washburn was Folsom's employer, Langford his friend, and the third member of the leadership team was Lieutenant Gustavus C. Doane. Doane headed a United States military escort, a much bigger operation in scale than the previous one limited to three men. Washburn had government clout because of his position, and Langford's enthusiasm had been stoked by Folsom and his speech in Helena.

Besides a taste for learning about the unknown, Washburn was motivated by the approval of Northern Pacific Railway construction and Montana state politics, which would play a role in the emergence of that railroad authorized by President Lincoln in 1864. The agreement to provide military accompaniment from Fort Ellis for the safety of the Washburn

Mule deer, elk, bears, sheep, bison—wildlife abounded in Yellowstone, as researchers past and present have always discovered.

party seemed welcomed by Washburn and Langford.

Although the names of Washburn and Langford were more prominently featured in the expedition title, several other civilians were in the party, including Samuel T. Hauser, who was then president of a Helena bank but later became governor of Montana Territory. Also in the group were Cornelius Hedges, who was attached to the United States Attorney's Office for Montana Territory and later wrote a series of articles about the trip for a Helena newspaper, and Truman Everts, who had previously been United States Assessor for Montana Territory. Everts became a singular figure in the early history of Yellowstone after he became lost, separated from the party for a lengthy stretch, was presumed dead, and then

was at the center of one of Yellowstone's legendary survival tales.

The Washburn Expedition included nine civilians in all; they departed from Fort Ellis on August 16, 1870, protected by a cavalry escort. They remained together until September 23, when the civilians rode back to Helena and the soldiers returned to the fort.

The route included time at Yellowstone Lake, viewing and naming many glaciers, as well as 10,243-foot Mount Washburn. Other mountains were eventually named after Doane, Hedges, Everts, and Langford. The difference between the Washburn Expedition and some of the earlier group visits to Yellowstone is that by 1870 these travelers understood much of what they were going to see. They might have been as spellbound by the spectacular nature of the scenery in person, but they knew it existed.

These were also notetakers, men who kept diaries, wrote articles and books, told the world what they saw, and no longer expected ridicule from their observations. Word was spreading that what seemed to be one-of-a-kind thermal features were located in Yellowstone, alongside many marvelous natural wilderness areas and, not to be overlooked, an abundance of wildlife.

Prior to this expedition, Montana's territorial governor Thomas Francis Meagher had publicly stated he believed the Yellowstone region should be converted into a national park. He may have been the first person to suggest such a move. However, in 1867, Meagher disappeared and presumably died when he fell overboard from a steamboat, making him unavailable to lobby Congress on behalf of the idea. Following the Washburn Expedition, it was Hedges who was an early spreader of the gospel that Yellowstone should become a national park.

Langford was also a vocal proponent of taking this major step. Langford wrote a slender volume about the expedition, though it was not published until 1905. By then many of the others had died and were not around to present other sides of the story as a reply to some of Langford's controversial content.

One thing in Langford's writing that did occasion discussion was whether or not he and others on the Washburn Expedition said: "Hey, we should work to turn this into a national park." At the least, this idea postdated Meagher's exclamation.

Langford had evidenced an interest in Yellowstone for several years and definitely was on the bandwagon for its creation as a park. In Langford's telling, the eureka moment when it was first proposed that Yellowstone should become a national park happened on September 19, 1870, while the group reclined in a camp where the Firehole and Gibbon Rivers meet.

Langford credited Hedges, who later put his thoughts into print, as the generator of the idea at that moment. Later, Langford said,

Washburn told him that prior to their leaving for Yellowstone, David Folsom, from the previous expedition, had suggested the establishment of a park at the Grand Canyon of the Yellowstone. Langford later wrote that Hedges did not know that when he tossed out his own suggestion. The truth may be that who said what first was murky, somewhat of a quiet buzz in conversation in certain circles. Certainly, John Muir was someone who may have made such a comment on any given day over a several-year period.

The Washburn Expedition chroniclers were quite impressed. At the 8,859-foot Dunraven Pass, Doane wrote of noting the rising steam from thermal features. "A column of steam from the dense woods to the height of several hundred feet became distinctly visible," he wrote. "We had all heard fabulous stories of this region and were somewhat skeptical as to appearances. At first it was pronounced a fire in the woods, but presently someone noticed that the vapor rose in regular puffs, and as if expelled with great force. Then conviction was forced upon us."

Welcome to the world of geysers. Doane wrote that the travelers let out a large group cheer. It was a solidification of truth about something that previously might have been considered fake. That evening, he said, members of the party followed up with closer viewings of thermal features.

Soon after, the expedition visited the Upper Falls and the Lower Falls of the Yellowstone. "Both of these cataracts deserve to be ranked among the great waterfalls of the continent," Doane wrote.

It was on September 9 when the group returned from its day's excursions and explorations that a head count showed Truman Everts was not present. This sparked consternation as the others sought to mentally retrace and replay how Everts could have been separated from his group.

Several of the men steered their horses back along the trail to search for Everts. As they traveled, they fired off signal guns, hoping to gain his attention. No response. They kept fires burning through the night at the camp as potential beacons. Only a limited amount of alarm initially pervaded the party because such an eventuality had been planned for with a Plan B standing in for a rendezvous at night camp. If a rider somehow split off from his group, he was supposed to meet up with the larger expedition at the hot springs located at West Thumb.

Members of the expedition realized that any number of things could have happened to Everts. He may have been attacked by either Native Americans or wildlife, fallen off a cliff, stumbled into water and drowned, or become so lost he could not find his way—or there might be some other explanation altogether.

What commenced was an early unexpected adventure in Yellowstone during which it seemed obvious with each passing day Everts might be dead. The expedition was located near the headwaters of the Snake River and the Yellowstone River. As everyone became certain Everts must be on his way to the West Thumb meeting place, after two days with no sign of him, the expedition moved there. When the all had arrived, there was still no Everts.

For the next week, forays were mounted seeking Everts, or at least seeking to determine what had happened to him. Yet no sign turned up and the party became steadily gloomier about the likelihood of a bad-news result. More focus was placed on finding Everts than exploration for four more days, through September 15. The situation became a bit more critical as the weather changed, growing harsher. Yellowstone, partially because of its elevations of six thousand feet and higher, can receive snowfall on any day of the year, and it does snow in the park, at least a little bit, twelve months of the year. During this stretch of time snow did come, and it amounted to about twenty inches of fresh precipitation. This made for harsher conditions for Everts to contend with and conspired against his survival.

Yet Everts was not dead. He endured a terrible ordeal, later written about in a piece called "Lost in the Yellowstone: Thirty-Seven Days in Peril." Everts penned it himself for the November

Even in winter, Yellowstone's scenery can be arresting.

1871 issue of *Scribner's Monthly*. A century and a half later, Everts's story is still considered to be one entrenched in the lore of Yellowstone and one in which man somehow persevered against the elements. More remarkable is that Everts was fifty-four years old at the time, during a period of American history when that was a somewhat advanced age.

Everts wrote there was nothing complicated about how he originally became separated from other riders and lost. On that fateful day, and others before it, they sought to penetrate very thick woods with downed trees impeding the way; each man made his own path he thought best. Although it was late afternoon and it was beginning to grow dark, Everts, who had his horse, was not worried and felt he would soon intersect with others again.

However, Everts was more lost than he believed. He had to pick his way carefully through the woods while periodically climbing off the horse and looking over the ground that lay ahead. When the forest was still too dense to negotiate and it became full-on darkness, he called it quits for the night, parked his horse, built a fire, and went to sleep.

His big error was failure to tie up his horse when he camped. The horse became scared and ran off, stranding Everts. This was particularly damaging because his blankets, gun, pistols, fishing equipment, and matches were stored on the back of the animal. Everts was left with some knives, the clothing he wore, and what he called a small opera glass.

An alarmed Everts spent half a day trying to catch his horse, but he could not. Then he set out again, on foot, in what he believed was the right direction to meet up with his partners. Here and there he left notes in case his mates stumbled upon his former positions. As time passed that second day Everts confessed to moments of fear and the sense of dread he had of sleeping out with neither food nor fire. Yet he always consoled himself with the fact he was sure he soon would be back with the other men. "I should soon rejoin my companions, who would laugh at my adventure," he wrote, "and incorporate it as a thrilling episode into the journal of our trip."

It became apparent quite soon there was little to laugh about involving Everts's predicament. He was not just around the corner from safety, not just over the hill from his fellow travelers. He was very much alone in threatening circumstances. He sought to maintain a good attitude despite the situation, writing, "When I began to realize that my condition was one of actual peril, I banished from my mind all fear of an unfavorable result." He tried to, anyway.

Everts casually noted he had a "timid" feeling about the dark and he was shrouded in pitch darkness. Each day he reached a point where it was not safe to push on. He then hunkered down for hours of listening to forest sounds, from those issued by birds to coyotes and wolves howling.

Everts's fear escalated the longer he was removed from other people and the more disoriented he became. He did not accurately recognize many of the comparatively few features of the park that had even yet been named. He also had to forage for meals with few weapons or utensils. He spoke of his despair when looking out upon a lake and seeing what he took to be a sail on a boat heading his way—certain to offer

rescue—only to have it turn out to be a pelican flying toward him.

"Oh, bitter disappointment," Everts wrote, "the object which my eager fancy had transformed into an angel of relief stalked from the water, an enormous pelican, flapped its dragon wings as if in mockery of my sorrow and flew to a solitary point farther up the lake. This little incident quite unmanned me."

Everts, hunger pains overwhelming some of the rationality of his thinking, had to search for a good sleeping spot as darkness descended again. During this search for a soft landing, he spotted a plant that appeared appetizing. He could not have guessed, but the thistle he alighted upon proved to be his salvation. "My appetite craved it," he said, "and the first meal in four days was made on thistle roots." As well as many afterwards. Indeed, thistle basically saved Everts's life.

That was one major problem remedied. Not so easily contended with was an encounter with a mountain lion. The animal roared at Everts and Everts screamed back, unable to scare it off for some time. When the animal finally darted off into the forest, Everts was overwhelmingly relieved.

When the weather turned colder and rain became snow, the inadequately clad Everts found himself picking a precise spot between two thermal features to use for heat as his resting stop. This reminded him that the worst of his situation was compounded by his inability to build a fire. He realized his feet were frostbitten, but then he burnt one of his sides when crust near a thermal feature broke and his body fell through to a steaming hot spot. Eventually, he somehow figured out how to make fires.

On and on Everts travailed. There was a forest fire and he burned a hand. He trekked to where he hoped he was supposed to rendezvous, always wondering if around the next bend he would find the other guys. Once, he became convinced he had gone the wrong way, two days' worth of travel. He was blocked from access to the Madison River by rock formations, and he

A full-curl ram checks out its surroundings.

could not bear the thought of turning around and retracing steps; such a move might break his fragile spirit.

Everts was entranced by the beauty of nature surrounding him, but he despaired of ever escaping it, saying, "How many dreary miles of forest and mountain filled the panorama!"

He then had a hallucination, seeing a ghost-like figure, who pointed the way back as the prudent direction to go because no food was in the area and the rocks were too much of an obstacle to ascend in his weakened state. It took more than four days for Everts to find food after he did turn around.

At times Everts wondered if the right choice was to simply stop moving and give up and die. Then his mind provided fresh hope and he continued on. He trapped a grasshopper, but could not catch trout to eat.

After time, the remainder of the Washburn Expedition went home, the soldiers back to the fort. But Everts was not forgotten. Search parties were formed and on October 10, three men from Helena came across the missing man near the Gardner River. He was crawling on hands and knees. It seemed miraculous to Everts, and even more so of a miracle when a member of the searchers said, "Are you Mr. Everts?" Everts replied, "Yes. All that is left of him."

The rescuers described Everts as reduced to skin and bones in stature, perhaps weighing only fifty pounds or so, and his clothes in tatters, almost unable to talk, and barely able to see.

One rescuer, "Yellowstone" Jack Baronett, thought a mountain lion was tracking Everts for a potential meal and perhaps the rescuers were just in time. Another, George Pritchett, said of Everts's appearance, "He is alive and safe, but very low in flesh. It seems difficult to realize the fact that he lived, but nevertheless, it is so."

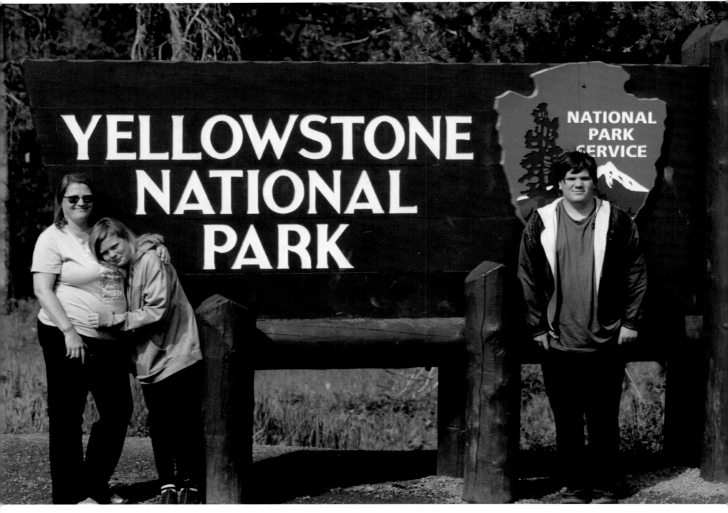

Signs like this one greet visitors at all entrances to Yellowstone National Park. Typically visitors like Alison, Britain, and Malachi Willis of Anchorage, Alaska, pose for pictures at the gateway locations.

CHAPTER 4
The Public Gets It

Truman Everts's death-defying solo journey through the wilds of Yellowstone contributed to the public understanding of the place, providing a fresh picture of its wildness. To a degree. Yet even in the 2020s, all members of the public don't always completely understand the risks inherent in the park.

Everts's dramatic tale, which enraptured its readership, built upon the mountain men's tales and the scientific explorations of the 1860s; the Washburn Expedition, too, helped craft the idea that this was a place that should be preserved, a place that should not be tampered with and eradicated.

One more major expedition put the Yellowstone-as-a-national-park idea over the top. This was the deal closer for the establishment of Yellowstone as a place to be saved. Ferdinand V. Hayden was both a physician and a geologist, and he led surveying expeditions through the American West. In 1871, Hayden mustered a $40,000 government grant to lead a fifty-person party into the Yellowstone region.

This was a serious commitment. Apparently, it was time, officially, to get the lowdown on what this place was all about. While Hayden's name was on the expedition's paperwork, some of the men who joined him on the trip were at least as important. Yellowstone had piqued more interest and was now beyond the point of merely having amateur, or even professional, mapmakers as the lead information providers. This journey upped the game by providing better visuals of Yellowstone's wonders, and indeed, the returns on many pictures illustrating the sights were immense.

Accompanying Hayden was painter Thomas Moran, whose works of Yellowstone scenery hang in prominent American museums today, and photographer William Henry Jackson, who snapped (black and white) pictures. Their artwork showed the masses what the firsthand visitors had only previously described.

This trip was also linked to whether or not a Northern Pacific Railroad would be built, so it was not solely altruistic work. By March 1871, when Hayden secured his money, Nathaniel Langford had delivered a well-publicized lecture in Washington, DC, focused on the Washburn Expedition. More attention for Yellowstone.

The bearded Moran, born in 1837, was a part of the Hudson River School of painting. He lived in New York City but was fascinated by the West, and he previously painted landscapes of the Rocky Mountains. He obtained full-time work for *Scribner's Monthly*, a prestigious illustrating job, and that helped propel his painting career. The connection between Moran and Hayden was made by wealthy financier Jay Cooke. Cooke had provided large sums of money to aid the Union Army during the American Civil War, and he was invested in the development of railroads. He was influential and was listened to when he spoke. Moran's addition to the group was to the benefit of all: his own career, the Hayden team, Cooke, and the American people.

A Civil War veteran, Jackson was an artist, too, before becoming a photographer in the infancy of the medium, with the goal of making a difference through his images. After trying his hand as a painter, Jackson, with his brother Edward's assistance, gambled on making photography his profession.

After a stint in Vermont, the siblings moved to Omaha, Nebraska, to start a business. Jackson got a break when he was hired to shoot pictures for the Union Pacific Railroad in the West, and that work gained him attention from Hayden.

On June 8, 1871, Hayden and his men, Jackson and his cameras, and Moran and his paintbrushes set off to make history in Yellowstone. The survey approached from the Gardner River area and journeyed past what is now Mammoth Hot Springs. Moran and Jackson were kindred spirits. Though working in different disciplines they shared an eye for detail and beauty and seemed to be on the same mission: seeing and recording the landscape, flora, and fauna offered by Yellowstone.

Hayden was particularly optimistic about the possible effect of Moran's work on the layman and the city dweller alike, and was enthused about his joining up.

"My friend, Thomas Moran, an artist of Philadelphia of rare genius, has completed arrangements for spending a month or two in the Yellowstone country, taking sketches for painting," Hayden recorded ahead of the journey.

While others were geologists and botanists, Jackson and Moran went about making pictures that would bring what they saw home with them and could be displayed in front of the uninitiated, who had only heard of the wonders of Yellowstone. While Moran could take notes, capture images with his eye and mind, and make sketches to expand upon later in comfort at home, Jackson was under pressure to produce then and there.

His process was tedious and quite physically demanding in that he was required to tote his equipment around on horseback. Jackson would have been astonished at the ease of how pictures are made in the twenty-first century, by the average Joe, on a cell phone (once he figured out what one was).

The crux of the matter was carrying around enormously heavy cameras and then developing the pictures for eight-by-ten-inch glass photo plates. This required delicate and lengthy work based on available lighting, as well as a washing and drying process, to make one picture. The

work had to be done at the spot, as well. It could not wait until Jackson got back to his studio.

One mishap with a mule cost Jackson. He lost a month's worth of photos in the accident, but despite his frustration retraced some of his steps to shoot the same sights over again. Among the pictures Jackson made were shots of Grand Teton and Old Faithful. Jackson brought the words of the mountain men, previously doubted, to life and demonstrated that these magnificent features were genuine.

Hayden may not have been as gifted an artist as Jackson or Moran, but he was a strong and loud advocate of Yellowstone becoming a national park. Congress had been presented with such legislation, and the groundswell of support was increasing. Hayden was also aware that the grand scenes of nature documented by Jackson and Moran were in jeopardy from despoilers eager to make profits, legally or otherwise, if the lands were not protected.

Hayden called these lurking figures "vandals" who were poised to destroy this "wonderland" crafted by nature over thousands of years. Hayden felt an urgency for Congress to act and protect Yellowstone. When he thought about a future without the area being turned into a national park, he worried.

Given humanity's propensity for development and resource extraction (especially that of Americans), and its seeming innate gene driving people in the direction of plundering over preservation, Hayden was right to fret, as would become apparent, even after Yellowstone became a park.

Post-expedition, Hayden and his team, Moran and his paintings, and Jackson and his photographs repaired to Washington, DC, where they staged lobbying efforts to convince enough politicians with no existing inclination to preserve to see things their way.

There was some suggestion Yellowstone be made a present to Montana by the federal government so it could administer it, much as what happened with Yosemite and California and the Yosemite Grant Act. However, a vast amount of the terrain, more than was contained within Montana, was part of Wyoming Territory. Since Wyoming did not become a state until 1890, this was a problem for some. It was determined the Grant Act should not apply.

Nathaniel P. Langford was an out-front supporter of making Yellowstone into a protected park. He made himself heard and strongly believed in the proposal. Moran was all for it, but he specialized in large paintings that took considerable time to complete, and much of his most famous Yellowstone oil painting work was not finished as Congress began deliberating. Everyone could gaze upon Jackson's photographs, though, once placed on display. They were exhibited in the US Capitol, and members of Congress studied them assiduously. Jackson lent them his eyes and brought the wonders to DC for their benefit—and the world's, as it turned out.

Moran and Jackson did serve up their own interpretations of many of the same places. It was said Moran visited thirty separate Yellowstone sites. He also kept a diary, and from the start, it was obvious how blown away he was by Yellowstone's beauty. One (casually ungrammatical) passage goes: "the route lay through a magnificent forest of pines & firs growing as straight as a ships mast & growing but a few feet apart, passed over the debris of a great land slide, where the whole face of the Mountain had fallen down at some time, laying bare a great cliff of five hundred feet."

It can be exclaimed some one hundred fifty years later that the very same type of scene can be seen in many areas of the park as the landscape shifts and stirs and rearranges itself. Although Moran painted images of great size and scale, he did manage to make a splash in DC with his first grand Yellowstone painting, *The Grand Canyon of the Yellowstone*.

The government liked it so much he was paid ten thousand dollars to sell it to the United States.

Sites such as pools of hot water were among the attractions for visitors to Yellowstone.

The equivalent cost in 2020 would have been roughly $213,000. The Department of the Interior took possession, and the painting is on semi-permanent loan for exhibit at the Smithsonian Institution. It is 84 inches by 144¼ inches in size, minus the frame. An individual more interested in obtaining a canvas wall hanging at the size of 26 inches by 32 inches for fun rather than the not-for-sale original can acquire a copy for $78.

When Congress took up the legislation for debate, one fact was ascertained that seemed to soothe the minds of some—no one was going to use the land for farming. It was also pointed out that no one really lived there (not counted were Native Americans, who had been active users of the land for thousands of years, though they had not established permanent settlements). However, there were individuals who had spent time in the Yellowstone area, claimed to be squatters at Mammoth Hot Springs, and wanted their ownership acknowledged.

A counterargument was made by one congressman, Representative Henry L. Dawes, saying a difference between the Yosemite deal and this one was that California gained jurisdiction of the former and the United States would maintain control of Yellowstone, so it could change its mind about its use. Still, Dawes did stress that since frost could be counted on every month of the year above seven thousand feet of altitude in that country, and it did, after all, contain "the most wonderful geysers ever found in the country," maybe agricultural development was not an issue. It may surprise many modern citizens that a US representative of the time raised the issue of whether the potential boundaries interfered with the Great Sioux Reservation.

The US House of Representatives voted 115 in favor of making Yellowstone a national park, sixty-five votes against, and sixty not voting. That had followed Senate passage, so the bill advanced to President Ulysses S. Grant for his signature.

Part of the legislation read thus: "An Act to set apart a certain tract of land lying near the headwaters of the Yellowstone River as a public park. Be it enacted by the Senate and the House of Representatives of the United States of America in Congress assembled, That the tract of land in the Territories of Montana and Wyoming . . . is hereby reserved and withdrawn from settlement, occupancy or sale, under the laws of the United States, and dedicated and set apart as a public park or pleasuring ground for the benefit and enjoyment of the people . . ."

The last phrase became the linchpin of the act in the public mind. It is the phrase that defines Yellowstone as being the people's park, owned by the people, a line uttered many times over as proof of what the government intended when it made Yellowstone a national park.

However, in the beginning, as the March 1, 1872, declaration took hold, Congress failed to appropriate any money to operate Yellowstone as a park. No funds at all. Anyone who thinks the creation of the National Park Service accompanied the first national park is dramatically mistaken.

The Roosevelt Arch marks the entrance to Yellowstone from the north side in Gardner, Montana. President Theodore Roosevelt is regarded as the first true conservation president.

The one action taken after Yellowstone became a park was to appoint Langford as its first superintendent, chosen by the Department of the Interior. Since Langford's first two initials were "N" for Nathaniel and "P" for Pitt, he picked up the nickname "National Park" Langford. In theory, this title should have made Langford very happy, since he was dedicated to the Yellowstone Park concept. But one of the other things overlooked by Congress was approving a salary for Langford to make a living at the job. Otherwise, this would have been a dream come true for him.

Instead, Langford had the marvelous title of superintendent and no power to exercise it. Since he still had to support himself, he basically lived elsewhere and had no time to regularly venture into Yellowstone. Langford's full-time job was as federal bank examiner for the territories and the Pacific Coast States. Yellowstone had no banks. More in line with how he spent his time, Langford roamed around promoting the need for a Northern Pacific Railroad. That would be deemed a conflict of interest today. Some suggested Langford's nickname to match his initials should have been "Northern Pacific" Langford.

As superintendent, Langford also had no authority to enforce the laws, such as evicting squatters, trespassers, or illegal hunters and trappers, because there were no funds to pay anyone to help him police the place.

Those most acutely interested in Yellowstone's preservation, who had labored hard to gain legislative passage of the act, became increasingly disenchanted with his performance. This was a bit unfair, since Langford had no tools to live up to his title. After five years of this peculiar management operation guided by Congress, Langford was ousted from the role.

Besides his journey with Hayden, it is said Langford actually only visited Yellowstone once during his tenure as superintendent. It was a valuable trip, though, in keeping with his authority. He evicted the man who had sought to have

A chance to see wildlife that could not be seen easily by residents of big cities (unless they went to a zoo) was also a lure for Americans—and later, foreign tourists.

his private squatter land grandfathered into the park and to stay in perpetuity at Mammoth Hot Springs. That was a no-go.

Others over the years sought to sneak into the park and poach wildlife, build their own shelters, and establish tourist businesses to make money in defiance of the Yellowstone preservation rules. There was a pervasive lawlessness at play in the park, and Langford was not equipped to cope with it shy of calling up the US Army. Ultimately, that was deemed the answer.

Regardless of the season, bison are likely to be viewed in herds spread across the landscape; they're especially numerous in the Lamar Valley.

CHAPTER 5
Wild and Untamed

Making Yellowstone a national park was one thing, but providing no staffing, rules, or playbook for operations meant the wilderness remained part of the Wild West.

There was also no route to reach the park for the people who were supposed to have the benefit of enjoying it. So the 1870s and beyond, for many years, were wild and crazy times in Yellowstone. That's where the railroad was supposed to come in—one day—to supply reliable transportation.

It took a while before the concept of Yellowstone as a vacation destination took hold in the minds of the public due to certain obstacles. One reason was the lack of transportation. Another reason was just how wild Yellowstone still was. A third revolved around the idea that the United States military, the cavalry stalwarts who had served in the Plains Wars, took command of the region.

Still, some people were intrigued from the start. Hard on the heels of those prominent late 1860s and early 1870s expeditions, small numbers of adventurous people did want to come. In 1873, one group took the dare and had the trip story published in their local newspaper. The reporter described the thermal features as "a million billion barrels of hot water" handy to make hot tea. "The tea was excellent," said Harry Norton, who also produced an early travel guide to Yellowstone, "and produced no disagreeable effects."

Geyser water was also used to boil meat, clean clothes, and wash dishes. A member of the party tossed dishes and knives into a geyser hole. At first he thought they were a lost cause, then watched them spit back up before once again seeing them all start to be sucked downward. One foolish participant kept grabbing at each

In the case of this particular animal, a group of tourists repeatedly took photographs from a reasonable distance under the belief it was a wolf. Experts identified the critter as a coyote eating dinner.

utensil that appeared, then shouted in pain from the intense heat warming the metal. Some of the culinary items were saved, though burned hands and fingers were suffered.

Most of the nation's Native Americans had been herded onto reservations as government policy by the approaching end of the 1870s, but not all. The military was sort of, kind of, in charge with their forts pockmarking the landscape. Yet that did not mean it was routinely safe for White people to be gallivanting about on horses and wagons at all times.

The government was anxious to take Sitting Bull into custody and retire the chief to a reservation. It was possible that as the Native American leader who had plotted the destruction of Lieutenant Colonel George Armstrong Custer and the 7th Calvary at the Battle of the Little Bighorn in 1876, Sitting Bull was the most hated man in America.

Moreover, in 1877, Sitting Bull led a band of Native Americans across the boundary into Canada, essentially seeking political asylum in what became Saskatchewan. The cavalry was also in hot pursuit of any other Native American groups that resisted turning in weapons and settling on a reservation, whether they had been warlike and opposed the government in battles or were peaceful. It was a one-size-fits-all policy. The goal was to transform the hunter-gatherer native peoples into farmers.

The Nez Percé Indians, under the leadership of Chief Joseph, wanted no part of the government's thinking; in 1877 some 750 members of the tribe were also on the run. For months, the Nez Percé stayed one step ahead of pursuing cavalry troops, leading them on a famous 1,170-mile chase. The Nez Percé, too, sought refuge in Canada, and rode as if their lives—at the least their way of life—depended on outlasting the troops. They traveled through Oregon, Washington, Idaho, Wyoming, and Montana, passing through parts of Yellowstone.

In its entirety, this episode was termed the Nez Percé War, although it was less a war than a very large manhunt. Newspapers followed this drama from afar, and at times promoted Chief Joseph into a noble figure, a superb military strategist, and a sympathetic individual. The pursuit through Yellowstone took place between August 20 and September 7, 1877, and this portion of the chase was very much a focal point, if only temporarily, of the entire incident.

The Nez Percé were not particularly interested in fighting with any of the White men they came across. They just wished to be left alone, to resupply and flee. But rather remarkably, history

This bison couldn't read the sign pinpointing his geographic location and was probably just a casual passerby.

shows there were eight or nine groups of tourists in Yellowstone at the time, most definitely roughing it. The Nez Percé came across several of these groups and conflict did arise. There were also prospectors illegally mining.

Despite the lack of amenities and the infancy of the entire idea of visiting Yellowstone for fun, some intrepid companies quickly got up and running and discovered there were some daring-at-heart individuals willing to check out the new national park and pay for the privilege.

Twice, the Nez Percé ran into touring groups, the Radersburg party and the Helena party. A Nez Percé scouting group led by Yellow Wolf captured John Shively of the Radersburg group near the Firehole River and forced him into a guiding role. They rounded up the tourist party and briefly held it hostage, then promised to release them all on the condition they leave their horses and supplies with the scouting group. However, a second, split-off group of Nez Percé intercepted them and demanded they remain in custody. Shooting broke out, and there were some casualties. Ultimately, even the wounded made their way into the hands of the cavalry.

There was more shooting when the Nez Percé came upon the Helena Party, and more injuries, though again most in the group were aided by the cavalry. Still, Richard Dietrich, who had taken shelter at a ranch building near Mammoth Hot Springs, stumbled into a smaller group of Nez Percé and was killed.

As the Nez Percé rode out of the park via Crandall Creek, heading toward the Clarks Fork of the Yellowstone River, the army was laying a trap designed to cut them off on the outskirts of Yellowstone. Trying to keep their location and route secret from the cavalry, the Nez Percé killed any hunters and prospectors they came across, thought to be ten in number.

To outflank the cavalry, the Nez Percé (numbering 750 people and two thousand horses, which left them significantly visible) shifted direction, more closely tracking the Shoshone River. They gained a vantage point high in the mountains, nowadays part of a road called the Chief Joseph Scenic Byway, from a spot called Dead Indian Pass. Instead of following an easier trail, they descended the rocky, dangerous route down Dead Indian Gulch. The narrow route offered difficult navigation, but it enabled the Nez Percé to throw the scent off their path and maneuver through thick timber and elude the soldiers.

Among the tribal members were just two hundred warriors, the rest women, children, and the elderly. Some had died in battles, others were worn down from fatigue and hunger, so there was a diminished number of Nez Percé fighters when the denouement came. First, there was conflict when the soldiers caught up with the group on September 13 in Montana. That fight did not end things. Onward the Nez Percé trudged. They did not quite make it to Canada before being headed off. The final showdown took place just forty miles short of the border in what is present-day Blaine County, Montana.

It was here that the matter was concluded when the Nez Percé officially surrendered on October 5. Chief Joseph made one of the best-remembered and admired speeches by a Native American leader, one that resonated in its plaintiveness across the country then and today. "Hear me, my chiefs!" Chief Joseph said. "I am tired. My heart is sick and sad. From where the sun now stands, I will fight no more forever."

An aside about the bloodshed from the civilian encounters with the Nez Percé in the park: The skirmishes were not especially good advertisements for tourism in Yellowstone. It could not have been a good souvenir to return home with a bullet wound in the head, as one tourist did. Several other people died while visiting the nascent park. The Nez Percé were not particularly seeking out the conflicts, but there were casualties while they were running for their lives.

Emma Cowan, her husband George, and her sister and brother were all members of the Radersburg Party. It was George who was shot in the head by the Nez Percé. Emma Cowan wrote: "The warm sunshine, the smell of blood, the horror of it all, a faint remembrance of seeing rocks thrown at his head, my sister's screams, a faint sick feeling, and all was blank."

Emma Cowan and her sister and brother were taken captive, but they were released two days later. George was unconscious and left behind. When he awoke he saw no one and was sure his wife was dead. "In about two hours, I began to come back to life," George Cowan later said, "and as I did so my head felt benumbed. The feeling as I can best express it was a buzzing, dizziness, and the sensation increased as it grew lighter and lighter. I found my face covered with blood and my hair clotted with blood that had cooled there."

Cowan then realized he was being watched by a Native American. After he struggled to his feet, he was shot again and plunged back to the ground. The shooter soon departed, leaving him to die. However, Cowan struggled back to movement and ended up crawling about twelve miles for help.

Once in the hands of the cavalry, Cowan was operated on by an army surgeon, who removed the bullet from his skull and returned it to him as a souvenir. He was pleased to learn his relatives were still alive, too. George Cowan kept the bullet from his wound as a watch fob for the

This grizzly was actually photographed outside Yellowstone, along the Buffalo Bill Scenic Byway on the way to the park from Cody, Wyoming. It took time out to scratch its back.

remainder of his life, one of the first and oddest tourism souvenirs of Yellowstone National Park.

It was obvious, even with only sporadic checking, that there was a certain element of lawlessness prevalent in Yellowstone National Park. It was all well and good that laws were passed in Washington, DC, naming Yellowstone protected territory; but Washington was far away, and the law on the ground was something altogether different.

To study the problems, in 1880 Harry Yount was assigned to spend the winter camping in Yellowstone to monitor its goings-on. He stayed in the park for fourteen months. Although there was no such thing as a park ranger at the time, Yount was a de facto ranger. The main problem he faced, outside of the possibility of freezing his toes off, was that there was only one of him to spread around 2.2 million acres of territory to observe. Even in modern times, with the use of a helicopter as an aid, that would be an impossible task.

Interestingly, although the government had appropriated no money to pay Nathaniel Langford as superintendent, eight years later Yellowstone had a budget of fifteen thousand dollars; one thousand dollars was earmarked for Yount's salary.

Yount was born in 1839, served in the Union Army during the Civil War, and was variously described as a mountain man, hunter, trapper, guide, and prospector after being hired by the Department of the Interior. His previous Yellowstone (and regional) experience included guiding for the Hayden Expedition.

During his year-plus stay in Yellowstone, Yount's primary assignment was to act as a gamekeeper, someone who tried to prevent poaching and wrote reports for the government on what he saw. Yount concluded Yellowstone was seen as fair game for many unscrupulous hunters and that far more protection was necessary than a solitary individual could offer.

Yount began work on July 6, 1880, and reported to the park's second superintendent, Philetus Norris, for whom the Norris Geyser Basin is named. Early on, Yount gave a park tour to Carl Schurz, the secretary of the interior. Yount established his own headquarters on the East Fork of the Yellowstone River (now Lamar River) in Soda Butte Valley, which is not far from present-day Gardiner, Montana.

It took little time for Yount to conclude Yellowstone needed more supervision and protection from poachers and tourists alike. In his first report, he wrote the park must have "the appointment of a small, reliable, active police force, to receive regular pay during the spring and summer, at least, when animals are likely to be slaughtered by tourists and mountaineers."

After the brutal winter of 1880–81, during which his thermometer broke, Yount filed another report, again concluding and stressing that more than just one man was needed to protect game. Enforcement of laws was needed on several fronts, he said, including guarding against "wanton slaughter" of wildlife and "careless use of fire" that could harm forests.

This on-site patrolling over an extended period, and his keen observations, were Yount's contributions to managing Yellowstone. Decades later, after the National Park Service was formed, he was praised anew. Horace M. Albright, the second director of the National Park Service, said, "Harry Yount is credited with being the father of the ranger service, as well as the first national park ranger." Albright made that point in his book published in 1928. Yount passed away in 1924.

Ultimately, after studying Yount's reports, government officials concluded he was correct in at least one area. They became convinced Yellowstone National Park needed broader law enforcement protection. While Yount wrote of policing, the solution came from a different source. The United States cavalry had roamed the Great Plains for decades, doing battle on horseback and operating out of fort headquarters in the Dakotas, Montana, Wyoming, and elsewhere. This could be a new realm of usage.

There were always going to be criminals on the loose. In 1886, fourteen years after

Yellowstone became a park without any staff to manage it, or money to pay for operating it, the War Department assumed responsibility.

Five years later, Fort Yellowstone was established at Mammoth Hot Springs within the park's boundaries. The aim was to staff it and use the men stationed there to enforce the rules in Yellowstone. This was an admission that the good intentions of Congress were one thing, but the good-heartedness of the people had its limits.

The cavalry operated out of temporary quarters until 1891, when the fort opened and the local headquarters became more permanent. No one knew how long the military would be in charge, but the construction teams constructed buildings between 1886 and 1913 at a cost of $700,000. What was total wilderness became a small city, with sixty buildings including barracks. They were built to last, many of them still in use more than a century later as office space and park administrative offices. The original phase of construction revolved around wooden buildings, but the later sandstone buildings were quite sturdy.

A focus of the military duties was horseback patrols throughout the park. The armed servicemen could deter poachers and other lawbreakers and protect the natural resources from wanton or careless destruction. This was a forceful government response to the illegal activities miscreants undertook under what they thought would be the cover of remoteness. It became much more difficult to get away with improper behavior with the army representatives lurking nearby.

While in twenty-first-century America it may not seem a natural match between the US Army and environmental consciousness, the first commanding officers in Yellowstone drew up their own set of regulations for preservation: they banned the cutting of timber, placed limits

In addition to its wealth of land mammals, Yellowstone features waterfowl of different types. Geese and ducks enjoy the numerous waterways inside the park.

on fishing, and governed the igniting of camp fires. The army also set up a system of regional cabins for the men to stay in while in the field, each about ten miles apart. Several rules revolved around common sense for behavior in the wilderness and became ingrained in operations across many national parks. In fact, the Yellowstone experiment was viewed as so successful that cavalry units were deployed in other parks as the park system expanded.

The first on-site military commander was Captain Moses Harris, who was awarded the Congressional Medal of Honor during the Civil War. His replacement was Captain Frazier Augustus Boutelle, whose lasting contribution was urging authorities to stock fish in many bodies of water to enhance the park's fisheries.

By all measure of historic reviews, the army was a successful steward of Yellowstone: on the spot when needed, innovative beyond the basics, and a bridge serving as park management between the days of lawlessness and the introduction of the National Park Service.

Several reasons led to the shift from the soldiers in charge to uniformed National Park Service personnel taking over. Park rangers were trained specifically for the job, with emphasis on enhancement of the skills necessary to survive in the wilderness, interaction with the public, and managing wildlife. In 1914, World War I began in Europe. By the end of 1917, the war had ensnared the United States, creating the need for all American soldiers' availability.

Some cliffs of Yellowstone glistening in the sunshine.

Kicking up some dust. Buffalo periodically drop to the ground and roll in the dust, called wallowing. They do so to scratch off fleas and bugs and, apparently, for fun.

CHAPTER 6
American Bison

Big heads. Elephantine, almost. Shaggy-haired, deep brown, wide-bodied, broad-shouldered, and horned, the animals are the kings of Yellowstone. Americans mostly call them buffalo, and science calls them bison.

They are the top-of-the-food-chain animal of most prevalence, regal and king-sized. Buffalo once roamed the Great Plains in the millions and millions, perhaps as many as sixty million. Once so commonplace that their number could only be estimated and not counted, buffalo were the wrong species for their time. Instead of being venerated, they were slaughtered. Instead of being viewed as a symbol of American wildness, they were nearly wiped out.

Animals majestic in bulk, impressive in number, and innocent of any inflammatory misbehavior, they were set upon for eradication as a by-product of an errant government policy combined with an eastern United States lust for warm fur coats, meat, inexpensive leather, clothing, paints, and pouches.

Although buffalo grow to between one thousand and occasionally two thousand pounds and are formidable animals to gaze upon, they present little threat to men because they are not carnivores, preferring prairie grass. They were not especially aggressive unless unduly harassed. Yet Americans went after them with a vengeance, determined to wipe them all out.

A major part of the buffalo's undoing in the late 1800s across the American West was the animal's symbolic and realistic importance to Native Americans. The American Indian revered the buffalo. The animal was part of religious culture while also being the great provider of so many things tribes needed to survive. Native Americans appreciated the buffalo, relied on it, and required

the buffalo as part of their diet, but also as part of their spiritual menu. Hunting buffalo was for needs, but also for ritual.

Often, when tribes cut treaty deals with the United States government (arrangements invariably broken by Washington, DC, representatives), a major part of the tribal thinking revolved around continued access to herds of buffalo to fulfill family food and clothing needs. Chiefs may have been uneasy about the treaties, but when they negotiated them they felt their fundamental needs were being protected if they ensured their tribes could still hunt buffalo. Then reality intruded, and the tribes were run off not only their traditional homelands, but also the substitute lands they were bestowed, lands they were told they would be able to hunt.

As much as anyone else in Native American authority, Sitting Bull hoped a meeting of the minds could take place and his Sioux people could survive the ever-growing pressure imposed by the White man. Always, whatever deal that had been made was abrogated.

"Only seven years ago," Sitting Bull said at one point, "we made a treaty by which we were assured that the buffalo country should be left to us forever. Now they threaten to take that from us also."

Sitting Bull didn't know the half of it. It was useless to make treaties that would inevitably be overturned by others focused on the devastation of the Native American. History showed whatever deals were made had no longevity and were never honored by the government; no one took the Native Americans' side even when it was clear they were in the right. The treaties were made because of expediency, but the Native Americans were a subjugated people who had no power to fight back or protest. They were essentially imprisoned on reservations, and their beloved bison were virtually eliminated.

Commercial hunting of buffalo was big business. It was attractive to those with an adventurous spirit and was vital to eastern industry, but it also served other purposes.

William F. Cody, the most famous American of his time, lived from 1846 to 1917. He was known from his work as a daring scout during the Plains Wars and worldwide touring with his Wild West exhibition. He was better known as "Buffalo Bill."

Cody earned his nickname because he was a buffalo hunter. He held jobs that required hunting meat for railroad construction workers, freight haulers, and cavalrymen stationed at western forts. By all accounts, Cody was a brilliant rifle shot who rode horses as savvy on the hunt as he was, and when he wasn't a scout he earned his living as a hunter. Cody figured he killed 4,282

buffalo on his assignments as a hunter, but this encapsulated only a short period of his life. He was busier much longer in show business than he was chasing down the animals on the frontier.

Men who killed buffalo for pay provided meat for many and hides and other parts of the bison's body to those who made leather and other products. Tanneries paid three dollars a hide and twenty-five cents per tongue from each buffalo.

Another prominent hunter, Tom Nixon, was said to have killed 120 buffalo in forty minutes in 1873, and 3,200 in just thirty-five days. Nixon made a show of the former event, witnesses watching atop a hill as he fired away.

While the sheer volume of buffalo killing helped the hunters make decent money, bison were not the hardest animals to hunt. They congregated in huge numbers and it took quite a bit of effort to stampede them. But they followed the leader, so if the hunter could get ahead of the lead buffalo he could steer the herd. (The suggestion

Peek-a-boo. It's not as if this slender tree can hide the massive beast lurking behind it.

here was that the buffalo were on the stupid side and did not react swiftly to imminent danger.) With a good horse it was possible to ride up close to the big beasts and unleash shots close up. A steady hand while in the saddle and using a big rifle that brought considerable power to the shots also helped a reliable man run up his total.

Far more offensive than those who killed the animals to support themselves, or to feed others, were the unconscionables who killed buffalo for sport and left them to rot on the prairie in the burning hot sun.

The White man gradually came to realize the buffalo's signal importance to Native Americans and in addition to the commercial hunters who wreaked havoc in great numbers on the animals for profit, the goal of eradicating buffalo became essential to the government's strategy of forcing Native Americans onto reservations, removing them from their traditional lands, and breaking them loose from cultural touchstones.

General Philip Sheridan was a strong advocate of this harsh policy, convinced eliminating buffalo would end conflict with Native Americans and the ends justified the means. "Let them kill, skin, and sell until the buffalo is exterminated," Sheridan said of the hunters, "as it is the only way to bring lasting peace and allow civilization to advance."

With the full weight of the government and the military behind Sheridan's outlook, no one had the influence to halt the buffalo slaughter. So the government, and its enforcement arm the United States Cavalry, were willing participants in developing an overriding scheme to separate American Indians from buffalo. A thorough way to accomplish this was by decimating the great herds. As much as the commercial hunters fed the demands of eastern buyers for horns, hides, meat, and other body parts to serve varying purposes, the government could have regulated the harvests to preserve the species. Instead, it was a key player in the gung-ho assault on the animal, with only a few small voices being overridden in their complaints of how man was destroying this magnificent species, virtually eliminating it from the planet.

A popular sight in spring is a mother bison with its newly born baby weighing perhaps fifty pounds.

This spring newborn baby bison is mastering the trick of how to walk on its own.

In 1874, recognizing the veritable criminal nature of this ceaseless destruction, Congress passed a law to make it illegal for any non-Native American to kill female buffalo; hunters were ordered not to kill any more buffalo than was needed to eat. However, it was nearly too late, and anyway, President Ulysses S. Grant vetoed the legislation. By the time anyone else stopped to listen, nearly all the buffalo were gone, killed and disposed of, hunted to near invisibility.

Almost, but not completely, too late in terms of extinction, the Lacey Act was signed into law by President William McKinley in May 1900;

otherwise the United States would likely have gone right on wantonly killing the species. It was too late for multitudes of buffalo, with their future teetering on the brink of no return.

The Lacey Act was the effort of Republican US Representative John F. Lacey of Iowa. The act protected wildlife, fish, and plants from being illegally possessed, taken, sold, or transported from their natural spots. It also gave the US Department of the Interior authorization to work to restore game and bird species that had been so dramatically reduced.

Lacey's efforts were partially in response to

the fate of the buffalo, but with an eye toward protecting many wild things that existed at the founding of the United States and were being threatened with extinction. "Man has been as wasteful of his natural possessions as the sun of its energy," Lacey said. "We have not been content with using these resources. We have wasted them as reckless prodigals. The annihilation of the noblest of all the American mammals is one of the crimes of the nineteenth century. Our children's children would curse us, and they ought to, if we do not prevent this reproach on the American people from being consummated. Today, there are as many millionaires in this city [New York City] as there are buffaloes in the whole world. The natural suggestion is that we are getting long on millionaires and short on buffaloes."

By 1900, it was estimated that fewer than one thousand buffalo remained alive across North America where once so many millions lived. Yellowstone National Park was one of the last holdouts of the few. In 1902, a government count discovered just twenty-three buffalo living within the park boundaries. Not so many years earlier the surrounding area might have been home to twenty-three million. That was the depth of the buffalo's woes.

Strangely, given its location, the National Zoological Park in Washington, DC, was also home to a fair number of buffalo, meaning government holdings were actually the supporting areas for about one hundred of the animals. Commonly referred to as the National Zoo, it is operated by the Smithsonian Institution. It was a great irony that many of the surviving American bison lived only down the street from the government offices where administrators developed plots to kill them off, and where legislators sought to save them.

As in the famous scene in the movie *Midnight Cowboy*, these uncensored bison take over Grand Loop Road in Yellowstone while announcing, "I'm walking here!"

If the bison of Yellowstone and the bison of Washington, DC, were lumped together for discussion purposes one hundred twenty years ago, that did not last. It was Yellowstone, with its abundance of space, as opposed to the nation's capital, with its abundance of automobiles, that became best known as the range the buffalo roamed.

By the early 1900s, in some quarters there was shame about how the United States had treated the buffalo. The American Bison Society was founded in 1905 through the energy and impetus of Ernest Baynes, William Hornaday, and President Theodore Roosevelt, who served as the nation's first conservationist president from 1901 to 1909. The society's aim was to prevent the buffalo from becoming extinct, a realistic threat.

This time period was the nadir for the buffalo. Even if the slaughter was over, the population numbers had dropped so low it would take a gargantuan effort to rebuild herds to any degree. As the United States grew and land was gobbled up by settlers, farmers, and westward dreamers, it was impossible for buffalo to regain their former territory.

The buffalo nickel (or Indian head nickel—one was portrayed on each side of the coin) made its debut in 1913. As currency, the coin was never a huge hit during the era it was minted, which was until 1938, but historically, and in fondness, the coin is one of the most popular ever made.

The artist behind the concept was sculptor James Earle Fraser, whose most famous work is *End of the Trail*, depicting a Native American slumped over on his horse. Fraser was sympathetic both to the American Indian and the North American buffalo, whose parallel plights were not lost on him.

The coin made a powerful statement for those who wished to take note of it, though there were many who didn't wish to be reminded of the sadness it portrayed. Even today, the complementary sides of American Indian and buffalo are moving. The nickel may not have been a gangbuster success in the US Mint's eyes, but it gave the thinking man a nudge in the right direction at a time when some seemed to be determined to do something to give a boost to the buffalo's future.

The American Bison Society worked on a small scale, with a dozen buffalo here and another dozen there, taken from zoos and then being donated to wildlife refuges and preserves, wilder places where they could be safe and thrive. Some

This bison decided to go for a stroll in the midst of a human crowd near Old Faithful. A ranger faithfully shouted repeatedly to get back—at the people.

animals from the Bronx Zoo were transported by train to Oklahoma, a most bizarre juxtaposition of residences for the animals.

Interestingly, in 1935, the society declared its work was done, its goal achieved of ensuring buffalo were saved and were not about to go extinct any time soon. That was an optimistic conclusion, though from a standpoint purely of extinction as opposed to continued growth, it was true. But in 2005, the organization was resurrected, back in business to help provide more assistance to the animal's future.

When it came to sheer numbers, the buffalo population grew steadily and kept expanding, especially on private ranches. It is possible that in the 2000s the animals became better liked than they ever had been and certainly became more admired and generally viewed favorably by the average citizen than they had been in about one hundred fifty years.

Protected as they lived within the confines of Yellowstone National Park, the two dozen remaining bison within the park very slowly regenerated, the population inching upward again as the decades passed. The herd, which of course did not respect manmade boundaries, in part wandered onto lands beyond the park's borders into Montana and Wyoming, as it ultimately reached as many as 5,500 bison.

This volume was considered to be too many for Yellowstone sustenance to adequately support and once again the government got involved in deciding how many bison should live and how many should die. This became a complex political question, especially in the 2000s, and what was agreed upon as an appropriate population limit for park living was set at about 3,600.

Sometimes, as a visitor to Yellowstone drives his automobile around the park, he comes across multiple herds spread out in the Hayden Valley, in the Lamar Valley, or simply dispersed along

Bison go where they want to in Yellowstone National Park and sometimes that means creating their own traffic jams, even if it means tying up automobiles or tour buses.

the road. He may think for a minute, or an hour, that he has been transported to the past when millions of the great animals ran free on the land, not merely thousands. The sight of hundreds in a single location, of thousands viewed in a day, is breathtaking enough. The imagination can barely digest the notion that once there were millions spread to the horizon, farther than the eye could see.

Dennis Lenzendorf is a retired National Park Service ranger who for years supervised the East Entrance to the park where visitors entered from Cody, Wyoming.

CHAPTER 7
The National Park Service

The style of wide-brim hat worn by National Park Service rangers at Yellowstone National Park, and throughout the rest of the country, stems from the days of the cavalry rider in Yellowstone during the era when the military presided over the 2.2 million acres of the world's first national park.

Rangers were trained in many facets of the outdoor work the military undertook, from enforcing the rules and arresting poachers to acting as tourist guides, or at least as the friendly cop on the beat, to point out what direction a visitor might follow to find Old Faithful.

Creation of the National Park Service in 1916 was a major step forward in the modernization of a formal staff as boots-on-the-ground representatives to supervise and protect national parks. The agency came into being through legislation called "The National Park Service Organic Act" and was signed into law by President Woodrow Wilson on August 25, 1916.

The enabling legislation encapsulated this assignment: "[The NPS] shall promote and regulate the use of the Federal areas known as national parks, monuments, and reservations" with the goal of their preservation "in such manner and by such means as will leave them unimpaired for the enjoyment of future generations." Just in case people forgot, they were supposed to enjoy the national parks.

National Park Service officials are part of the Department of the Interior, and there are approximately 12,500 employees (a sharp increase from the days of Nathaniel Langford and Harry Yount). By 2020, there were sixty-two national parks, but 419 entities that came under the heading of supervision by the National Park Service.

It was obvious from the earliest days of Yellowstone, when the park was established with no budget and no personnel, that if the mission set by Congress was to be achieved, there needed to be people on site for preservation. It took decades, however, to pass through the stages from no oversight to military oversight to government oversight.

When government approval came with the act, it was the culmination of conservationist lobbying, much of it attributed to a prominent businessman named Stephen Mather. After President Wilson's signature was affixed to the bill and steps were taken to organize the National Park Service, Mather became the first director. He started May 16, 1917, and remained in the position through January 8, 1929.

Mather was the man who truly got the National Park Service going and developed the core principles of attracting tourists as a method of protecting parks themselves. Mather believed the more people who came and saw the wonders, the more they would spread the word to friends and relatives telling them to visit, and based on their own experiences would also become more invested as park supporters.

Born in San Francisco in 1867, Mather was a millionaire businessman and an early conservationist. While living in New York before entering the business world, Mather was a newspaper reporter. A good friend from those days was the journalist Robert Sterling Yard, and the duo worked together to promote the idea of a necessary National Park Service. The men were not only like-minded; their relationship was close enough that Yard was the best man at Mather's wedding.

Mather first worked for Pacific Coast Borax Company under his father in New York and at the company's many offices across the country. He coined the famous advertising campaign that endured for decades and was well-known to certain generations of Americans for the brand 20 Mule Team Borax.

Eventually, bouts of bipolar distress and mental illness drove Mather from the business world. Although these afflictions would interfere with his health for the remainder of his life (he died in 1930), Mather used his time to become involved in different conservation groups, from the Boone and Crockett Club to the Sierra Club. He eventually became assistant secretary of the Department of the Interior and began his lobbying effort favoring a government agency to administer the park system.

This included hiring Yard as a publicist to sell the idea to the public. Mather spoke and Yard

Yellowstone fisheries biologist Todd Koel steering a National Park Service boat on Yellowstone Lake.

wrote. By the time the National Park Service was created, there were fourteen national parks and nineteen national monuments. Always, Yellowstone was the center of attention, partially because it was the first entity, partially because it was the most prestigious, partially because of the hold it had on public imagination. Given the original lack of appropriation for Yellowstone, it is intriguing to note that by the time Horace M. Albright succeeded Mather as the second National Park Service director, the department's budget had grown to $9 million.

Selling congressmen and the public on the need for a new government agency was a long-term battle, with legislation introduced each year between 1911 and 1915 urging formation of the new agency, only to fail to gain a majority in Congress.

Another of Mather's allies in this struggle was Frederick Law Olmsted Jr., the son of the man who designed New York City's Central Park. Olmsted Jr. participated in the writing of the legislation that became the National Park Service law. It was difficult to tell the difference between the words Mather spoke and those Olmsted penned into a bill, again the emphasis being on the responsibility of the National Park Service to "conserve the scenery and the natural and historic objects and the wildlife therein."

Mather's main partner at the National Park

Todd Koel, the chief fisheries biologist in Yellowstone National Park, is heavily involved in cutthroat trout restoration and in protecting the fisheries resource.

Service was Albright. The two men began working together in Washington, DC, even before the service was approved. Albright was assuredly Mather's right-hand man. He was his chief assistant and considered Mather his mentor. For a time, Albright was shipped from the headquarters of the bureaucracy to serve as superintendent of Yellowstone. Any time Mather was incapacitated by illness, Albright filled in. Eventually, in 1929, he succeeded Mather as director, serving until 1933.

Mather and Albright were kindred spirits and the ultimate boosters of the national parks; they brimmed with ideas that would lure more and more tourists to the parks in general and Yellowstone in particular. In a sense, Yellowstone, the most famous of the parks, served as an incubator for ideas. Plans that might well serve all were tried in Yellowstone first.

Mather said the parks had to be preserved in their natural state as much as possible, but it was very important they be accessible, not placed on some pedestal. They were to be used and enjoyed by the people. "All other activities of the bureau must be secondary," Mather said.

Fundamentally, Mather and Albright agreed on the more-the-merrier philosophy, strongly backing ideas that would bring more city dwellers to the wild to be introduced to nature. That was one reason they supported access to Yellowstone by train travel. Unlike those mountain men of the past, the average American in the 1920s United States was not going to ride into the grand park on horseback. They might like to take a day trip on a horse for the adventure of it all while there, but they were not going to carry along luggage from Philadelphia by pack horse.

It was obvious from a certain period on that the American tourist may well appreciate the wilderness of the national parks and the very wildness of Yellowstone, but while visiting he wanted a certain level of comfort in a hotel and wanted to be able to order a fine meal. Otherwise hotels like the Old Faithful Inn and the Lake Hotel would not have been built so early.

The Old Faithful Inn lobby and its earliest rooms went up in 1903–1904, and the building has become an institution as visited as the Old Faithful Geyser. Those who come to watch the spray feel obligated to at least step inside the building and gaze at the high ceiling, the magnificent wooden structure, and the huge fireplace. Getting a reservation to stay there is another matter, a different challenge, even at close to three hundred dollars a night.

National Park Service ranger Brian Perry succeeded Dennis Lenzendorf as the supervising ranger at Yellowstone's East Entrance.

That was not the price when the sparkling Lake Hotel opened on the shore of Yellowstone Lake in 1891. Currently, this is the oldest operating hotel inside the park's borders. There was work done on the building over the years, quite dramatically when it was completely renovated between 1984 and 1990 and in recent years when wings were altered in the 2010s. Hotels such as the Old Faithful Inn and the Lake Hotel help provide the complete Yellowstone experience with their deep roots in history, but they are not for everyone's budget.

Mather and Albright very much wanted Yellowstone as a whole, and the national parks as a group, to be within anyone's budget. They wanted families to be able to afford the entrance fees on summer vacations.

When Mather was trying to sell the proposal of founding a National Park Service he traveled thirty-five thousand miles by train and automobile—he drove his early Packard—as a lobbying evangelist. He was a true believer in conservation and the parks' mission. As an independently wealthy individual, he could also invest the necessary time in the cause. He gained support from various organizations, John Muir's Sierra Club and the National Geographic Society among them. In fact, after the National Park Service was created, the National Geographic Society made an $80,000 donation in seed money, an enormous amount for the times, but something that would be illegal under today's laws.

Mather came to his task equipped with a wide range of ideas, though there was again some congressional dilly-dallying between the adoption of the law and its implementation with the slow-moving body not committing any start-up funds for eight months. That must have been a frustrating time for Mather, and it accounts for the gap between President Wilson signing the measure and Mather assuming the rank of National Park Service director.

Park rangers are instantly recognizable, even from a distance in national parks, because of the uniforms they wear. The hats may resemble the old military-style tops, but the uniforms have a quasi-military look as well. Mather's goal for rangers was not so much to appear as police enforcers as to possess an official look. Enforcement, though, was very much part of the job, especially in the wilder days of Yellowstone and other parks.

Above all, when it came to the National Park Service, Mather wanted to instill from the start an aura of professionalism. Above all, he felt powerfully that the national parks needed protectors against would-be despoilers. One writer bluntly stated the National Park Service's number one task was to make certain no one wrecked Yellowstone and the other treasures: "The first job of the new National Park Service was to save the parks from the exploitation schemes already undertaken."

Mather took great pride in the work rangers did, whether they were enforcing the law against poachers or simply being helpful in answering tourists' questions. Although his office was in Washington, DC, at the seat of government, Mather enjoyed venturing out to the parks he was supervising. The highly ranked government official would anonymously sidle up to a group being addressed by an interpretive ranger and make like an interested passerby and eavesdrop on what was being said.

Indeed, when Albright wrote a book called *Oh, Ranger!*, he asked Mather to produce an introduction, and the very first words his predecessor wrote were: "To me, no picture of the national parks is complete unless it includes the rangers, the 'Dudes,' the 'Sagebrushers,' and the 'Savages.' I like to picture the thousands of people gathered about the park campfires, asking questions of rangers. . . . They are a fine, earnest, intelligent and public-spirited body of men, the rangers." (The rangers were all men in 1928 when the book was first copyrighted, though women long ago joined the profession.)

It should be noted, even if it was not by Mather, that often enough the naïve nature of many of the questions rangers are asked border on the silly and absurd. Albright began his book with an example of one of those kinds of questions. "Oh, Ranger," it reads, "can I take your picture with a bear?"

Somehow, from the beginning, the tourist from far away got mixed up and came to believe a national park was a synonym for a zoo, that they would always be safe from the animals because they were probably domesticated as if behind zoo bars. Reality never entered the minds of many.

Of course, there was a time period when rangers, as part of their duties, were required to feed the bears. Not by hand, it should be noted, but there was a meal time of garbage on a daily basis.

Welcome to Yellowstone. That is the greeting offered by National Park Service ranger Brian Perry when visitors drive up to the East Entrance. He hands them maps of the park and a park newsletter, as well.

Rescuing visitors, directing people to camp sites, fighting fires: the park ranger has one of the most multifaceted jobs in the country. "All in a day's work" was a phrase regularly uttered, but when they awoke for their shift that day, none of those performing service for the NPS knew what the day might bring, which one of those tasks they might be involved in.

The earliest tourists to Yellowstone ended up risking their lives by walking into conflict between the US Cavalry and the Nez Percé. Railroads, seeing there was money to be made, got into the act and began transporting visitors to Yellowstone from hundreds and thousands of miles across the continent.

By 1882, train service on the Northern Pacific delivered passengers to Livingston, Montana, which is not far from Yellowstone, but not quite in the neighborhood. It is fifty-four miles from Livingston to Gardiner, Montana, where the north entrance of the park is located. By 1902, train service reached Gardiner and transfers were made to stagecoaches to ride into the park. By 1908, train service was added to West Yellowstone, Montana, where the community abuts the West Entrance.

The world was changing and maturing, and in 1915 Yellowstone authorized people to drive their own automobiles into the park. By then, an individual, with belated fanfare, illegally drove into the park just so he could say he was the first. Officially, though, the first car in the community of West Yellowstone was purchased by a man named Sam Eagle and for $7.50 he was sold the No. 1 park permit. Only the first five miles of the park road from the West Entrance were paved back then.

The arrival of cars was certain to spell the death knell for stagecoaches, and indeed there were early conflicts between auto drivers and wagon drivers as the horses became frightened, flared up, and objected to the noises made by the vehicles.

However, any change or development that would bring more people to Yellowstone or to any national park was a good thing in Mather's mind. Most assuredly, once Yellowstone became the first national park, people took note. It was not easy to get to, had no amenities, was the embodiment of roughing it, and yet there was curiosity.

Official statistics for attendance at Yellowstone in 1872 say three hundred people came during that debut year. By 1877, it was one thousand; five thousand in 1883; close to eleven thousand in 1897; and it stayed above five figures after that. By the time the National Park Service was on the verge of approval in 1915, the attendance was 51,895. An immediate drop-off was felt during World War I, but as soon as hostilities ceased the visitor count mushroomed. The first six-figure year was 1923 with 138,352 visitors. The cumulative total from the time the park opened over the first fifty-year span topped one million.

Clearly, enough people cared about Yellowstone National Park to make the trek. Mather was a proselytizer, a preacher for the parks, someone who thought the body and mind benefited from exposure to them. He never wearied of promoting the parks from the standpoint of their being part of America's good fortune.

"Who will gainsay that the parks contain the highest potentialities of national pride, national containment, and national health?" Mather said. "A visit inspires love of country; begets contentment; engenders pride of possession; contains the antidote for national restlessness. It teaches love of nature, of the trees and flowers, the rippling brook, the crystal lakes, the snow-clad mountain peaks, the wildlife encountered, everywhere amid native surrounding. He is a better citizen with a keener appreciation of the privilege of living here who has toured the national parks."

The roughly 5000 bison in the park today are descendants of two dozen that escaped extermination by the US military in its war against the tribes that depended upon them.

CHAPTER 8
The Grizzly Bear

The Wild West was home to the grizzly bear, a beast that seemed to come with its own fully formed history and mythology as an animal to be feared and respected.

With big teeth and long claws, a roar that could shake a man to his soul, and formidable size that varied in the telling (one day he was described as 1,000 pounds and the next 1,500 pounds), the grizzly, or brown bear, fascinated easterners who visited Yellowstone National Park, a place where bears lived in fair abundance.

Since the animals had no map-reading skills, they were not bound by the park's boundaries and populated the rest of the West from California eastward through the Rocky Mountains. The Lewis and Clark Expedition brought home tales of the big animals, mostly stories relayed through Native American tribes, but occasionally through some first-person contacts that scared the jelly out of the men on the journey.

Bears may have traveled on four feet, but when stretched to full height on back legs, they were said to be eight feet tall. Unlike many other species of wildlife, they did not necessarily readily scamper away upon sensing humans in the vicinity. Sometimes yes, other times no. If the bears put their minds to it and charged, they were a frightening sight and instantly put lives in jeopardy. A single shot from a black powder gun might not even slow an enraged bear, never mind kill it.

Forget those four-figure weights; a bear weighing even hundreds of pounds less could make an impression on a man. Lewis and Clark famously kept meticulous journals of the expedition's trip and that included noting bear encounters.

One such meeting took place on May 5, 1805. Meriwether Lewis was the notetaker who said a bear estimated at a weight of around six hundred pounds was called a "most tremendous looking animal and extremely hard to kill." Clark, who was not the best speller in the world, gazed upon the creature and wrote of the grizzly that it was "verry large and a turrible looking animal." Clark, assisted by another expedition member, shot the bear ten times before it died.

This was a new experience for Lewis and Clark. They had been warned by Native Americans that tribal members would not tackle a grizzly unless they had a mini-army of six to ten warriors on hand. The first bears the expedition ran into were on the small size, and they gave the impression that they weren't so hard to kill after all, and maybe the stories were all exaggeration.

It turned out it was all a matter of scale, and Lewis had an additional experience after a buffalo hunt that showed him a big bear was a different animal, so to speak. After shooting the buffalo, Lewis had not yet reloaded his rifle, so he was basically defenseless when a bear came running at him. He followed the strategy of making a quick retreat. It was flat and open ground with no trees. Lewis was near a river, however, and ran into the water. The bear came in, as well, but then changed its mind, apparently determining Lewis was not worth the trouble of a swim.

Lewis and Clark, the co-leaders of the Corps of Discovery, then adopted the safety policy of telling their men not to walk in the woods alone. However, expedition member Hugh McNeal was riding a horse solo on July 15, 1806, when a bear surprised rider and horse. The horse reared up and tossed McNeal, leaving him on the ground near the bear. There was no time to aim his rifle, but McNeal wielded it as a club, smacking the bear in the head and slowing it down. While the

Grizzly bears, mostly adult males, can weigh more than one thousand pounds; they are the apex predator in Yellowstone.

bear sought to recover, McNeal climbed a tree. Although black bears are adept at tree climbing, grizzly bears are not as proficient. McNeal was no expert on this analysis, but figured he could wait out the bear's patience with his own, especially with his life potentially in the balance.

For the time being McNeal was okay, protected by his perch. But the bear was evidently mighty ticked off and very patient. Hours passed and the bear did not leave the scene. McNeal hunkered in the tree. When darkness arrived, the bear finally gave up and McNeal was at last able to climb down and find his way back to the expedition's camp, where he reported in.

In the end, the Corps of Discovery, which maintained a tremendous record of avoiding casualties overall, did not suffer a loss to a grizzly bear, and Lewis, with his newfound respect for the animal's prowess, thought that represented very good fortune. "The hand of providence has been most wonderfully in our favor," he said.

Bear attacks on humans have been irregular occurrences over the last couple of centuries, in both Yellowstone and the surrounding area; they are meticulously documented when they occur. While a healthy wariness is warranted at all times, and was in the early 1800s, as well, the number of grizzly assaults and fatalities of people can only be summed up as a rarity. Man is correct to be scared, because there is every chance an encounter can turn sour; logic and preparation can only do so much.

From the beginning of time people were the predators, applying superior brain power to their hunting approaches. So they are always spooked when they become prey, when they no longer

This grizzly took up a perch downhill from the road on the Buffalo Bill Scenic Byway on the way to Yellowstone National Park.

have the upper hand in the face of a more powerful animal, whether it be a grizzly bear or a great white shark. Although those shark encounters are definitely pretty rare in the woods.

The grizzly is the animal big enough, strong enough, and unpredictable enough to go where it wants to go, when it wants to go there, and if a person happens to be in the way, he had better vacate the path or risk being maimed or killed.

It is also true that from the beginning one reason tourists wanted to visit Yellowstone National Park was to see bears up close. They did not want to sacrifice their lives for the privilege, but they wanted the excitement of being in proximity

and telling the family and neighbors back home about seeing one. In fact, in Stephen Mather's mind, the closer the viewing the better, even if physical contact was involved (as long as it was not fatal). Yellowstone tourists became so enamored of the bears they completely forgot they were wild animals and on a regular basis tried to hand-feed them cookies or peanut butter and jelly sandwiches. Sometimes the happy creature took a larger bite than was anticipated and drew some blood on the hand that fed them. Anytime a visitor complained about such an incident, Mather downplayed it, saying a little scar simply made for a better souvenir of Yellowstone than

This pair of grizzlies made itself at home along Grand Loop Road chowing down on vegetation even though dozens of tourists were close by snapping pictures.

Off to find more food, these bears wander away from crowds of people anxious to make souvenir photographs.

others brought home. That's a guy who thought on the bright side.

In the earliest days of the National Park Service, the paramount mission in Mather's head, beyond the overriding, fundamental one of preservation, was increasing attendance in Yellowstone. The bears were a major attraction and for many years ranger duty included a regular daily feeding show.

The bear feeding chore overlapped with garbage disposal at park hotels. A temporary but years-long solution was to haul the hotel's waste to a specific area that was nicknamed "the Lunch Counter." Inside a loosely constructed corral, bears gathered for a feeding session.

Bears will eat just about anything, such as tree bark and roots, squirrels, rotting meat on wildlife carcasses, and garbage produced by humans. The area called "the Lunch Counter" also had signage reading, "For Bears Only." It was not as if people were going to indulge in this buffet, and other animals could not read, so the words were really part of the advertising package for the visitor who traveled one thousand miles to see bears and by golly was going to get that chance if the National Park Service could provide it.

Bleacher seating was even erected for the comfort of guests for the end-of-the-day feeding sessions. Since there was enough for all, grizzly bears and black bears both showed up to chow down without battling over the goodies. They slinked into the feeding zone at dusk and ate their fill. Who says there is no free lunch?

This was definitely a highlight of the bears' day. Rather than hustle and forage for food, they could count on being presented with free meals. However it was communicated within the species, the word spread, and between 1920 and 1930 the regular number of bears that turned out for the garbage dispersal expanded from forty to two hundred fifty. Likely, new generations of bears were just raised that way, following mama to the feeding ground and never realizing this was not typical behavior in the bear world at large.

At the height of this reckless operation, a few visitors each night could ride along on the small hotel garbage cart and get right up next to the bears when the "food" was handed out.

This regular procedure, though, resulted in problems. Bears became more and more habituated to humans. They also became greedy. They were not content to wait all day for the feeding. Rather than being typically reclusive around people, they would emerge from the forest and rush out onto the park roads. Of course, the drivers came to a stop to obtain close-up photographs of the bears, to feed them, and in some instances, to foolishly pet them. Difficulties arose when the people ran out of food and the bears had not yet run out of appetites. They wanted more and they devolved into bad moods when there was no more to be had. They began rocking cars, reaching in through open windows and grabbing at people, and breaking windshields. Far from a feel-good encounter with bears, the visitors grew frightened. They put themselves in jeopardy.

It took many years before the practice of feeding the bears garbage was eliminated, and the last garbage dump was closed in 1970. Policy in place these days is to warn visitors of the dangers of mingling with bears by issuing regular reminders on the park website, in brochures, and on flyers handed out upon entering, all forcefully explaining what might go wrong if the rules of safe social distancing are not followed.

While it was a gradual process, education of the public has also gone a long way toward keeping people and bears separate from one another, although their paths do overlap on hiking trails within Yellowstone and most definitely within the broader Greater Yellowstone Ecosystem that encompasses the surrounding areas.

Bison may have offered the most visually overwhelming views of large animals on the Great Plains and in the Rocky Mountains, but going back as far as the Lewis and Clark days, bears were regarded as the most menacing inhabitants, with the larger grizzly carrying a much more significant aura than the smaller black bear.

It will likely shock many that in the one hundred fifty years that Yellowstone has been a park, there have been just eight human fatalities blamed on grizzly bears. Geysers and their intensely hot steam and boiling water have accounted for many more deaths.

One study indicated it is almost as likely for a person to be killed by a falling tree or an avalanche or, yes, from being struck by lightning in Yellowstone than to be killed by a grizzly. Record-keeping indicates the extraordinary rarity of humans killed by bears within the park's boundaries.

One reason the bears of Yellowstone are so popular is because the number of bears in the wild underwent dramatic population shrinkage as the nation expanded westward, staking out new cities and expanding its population. Scientists have estimated that between 1850 and 1920 bears disappeared from 95 percent of their original range in the United States. Only about 2 percent of the original bear range in the country now remains for bear habitat.

Other highly publicized cultural developments contributed to the formation of the grizzly bear as an animal of great curiosity. The connection between President Theodore Roosevelt and the creation of the teddy bear stuffed animal in

1902 brought wild reams of attention to bears in a kid-appealing manner. Roosevelt was an avid conservationist, but also very much a hunter. He went on a black bear hunting trip to the Mississippi Delta on a patron's property. Dogs were employed to sniff out the bears for this hunt and Roosevelt's famed guide, Holt Collier, set him up in an advantageous position.

However, bears, dogs, and people moved around. A 250-pound bear grabbed the guide's favorite dog until Collier intervened and clobbered the bear. Roosevelt was summoned to make the kill of the woozy bear, but refused to do so. He said it would be unsporting to do so in its weakened state. When word spread, public opinion skewed heavily in Roosevelt's favor of choosing such a tack. Editorial cartoons exploded in newspapers across the land. Soon after, a toy manufacturer began making stuffed bears and they gained the name the "Teddy Bear." While it may not be widely known that there is such a

designation, as a result of this incident, the state toy of Mississippi is the teddy bear.

Bears were getting good press. Also around this time, published in 1900, *The Biography of a Grizzly*, written by Ernest Thompson Seton about an orphaned bear named Wahb, became a huge hit. The unusual story was written in the first person from the point of view of the bear.

A 1903 story chronicling a family journey to Yellowstone dealt with another such Seton character, Johnny Bear. The author noted, "The children know 'Wahb' and 'Johnny Bear' by heart, of course."

So in some ways the bear developed a contradictory image as somewhat warm and fuzzy, yet also fearsome.

Many of the early visitors to Yellowstone did bring supplies with them, but they also planned to hunt and fish for food. One traveler wrote out a lengthy list of the kind of meat that was available as long as you killed your own. Itemized as

This type of sighting of a grizzly in Yellowstone is acceptable—unless the bear decides to narrow the distance.

potential main-course menu choices were buffalo, moose, elk, bear, wolverine, black and whitetail deer, antelope, and so on. He wrote, "[A]ll could be gotten within five miles of our camp and in a very short time."

However, this fellow did discover, as did the Lewis and Clark journey members, that seeing a grizzly bear and harvesting one were two different things. Bears were seen just about every day by this visitor, but one day a specimen seemed to be blocking the way near the Lower Geyser Basin. Despite a warning from his guide to let it be, the man decided he just had to shoot it.

Advancing to within seventy-five yards of the bear, the man pointed his rifle and fired. "Down went the bruin to the ground with a terrible growl. It was up again and to my great surprise there was at her side a large cub." He reloaded and fired again, but the scene had descended into madness, with the guide trying to control horses in the face of a now-enraged bear. "The infuriated monster made direct for me," the hunter said. The only thing that saved them all was a creek the bear had begun to ford. But the bear changed its mind and stopped following. After the tension subsided, the rather angry guide told the tourist if he went after another bear on the trip, he hoped the man would be eaten.

That was probably said merely in the heat of the moment, but unfortunately such things have happened.

Yellowstone's history shows that deaths from grizzly attacks were recorded in 1916, 1942, 1972, 1984, 1986, twice in 2011, and in 2015. A 1909 book discussed an incident where it was claimed a man poked a bear with an umbrella and the ticked-off bear then killed him. The park has no record of this happening, though, and no newspaper clippings of such an event were found by researchers.

Still, many more individuals have been killed by bears across North America—in Alaska, Canada, elsewhere in the American West, and even on the outskirts of the park within the Greater Yellowstone Ecosystem.

Over the last one hundred years, many bears may have adopted ranges that take them beyond park boundaries, into areas nearby, and even back into the park.

Going way back in time, a documented black bear kill in New Hampshire of an eight-year-old boy dates to August 1784. In the 1850s, there were some documented grizzly, or brown bear, kills where hunters wounded bears, but the bears finished them off before they could do the same. Also commonly reported, and one of the most dangerous of situations for humans in the backcountry, are cases where people stumbled upon a mother with cubs who attacked the people as a protective move.

Most of Yellowstone National Park is located within the borders of the state of Wyoming. Wyoming was a territory when the park was founded and became a state in 1890. The first recorded fatality by bear in Wyoming after it joined the United States occurred in 1892 and was a strange tale.

A man named Phillip Vetter, thirty-seven years old, was killed near the Greybull River. The week before he was found dead on September 2, 1892, Vetter, who was a buffalo hunter, told another hunter he was headed into the woods to hunt bears. Soon after, a different hunter, who was in the forest in a rainstorm, saw Vetter's cabin and, hoping to get dry, entered the structure. The inside had been ransacked by a bear and Vetter lay dead.

The surprised searcher saw a newspaper with blood on it. Vetter had scratched a message indicating he had been in a fierce fight with the bear, was bitten and clawed, and wrote, "I'm dying." The hunter came across Vetter's hat and rifle, with a bullet stuck in the chamber, but also two empty casings. If Vetter had fired, there was no true proof. There was no bear around. Ultimately, Vetter was buried at the Old Trail Town historical tourist site in Cody, Wyoming, where the remains of the real-life John "Jeremiah" Johnson are also interred.

Even men who were prepared could die by the claws and teeth of grizzlies, including a US

Mostly, when bears show themselves to the public they are on the prowl for good eats and don't want to be bothered as they dine.

forest ranger and a Canadian game warden. Those were events in the wild, but in the 1930s there were at least three cases of zookeepers being killed by bears in their charge and another situation when a gas station operator who kept a bear in a cage was killed. A man died from the weight of being crushed by his own pet bear that had no claws or teeth during a wrestling match at Fort Leonard Wood in Missouri. In a famously dissected occurrence, two young women in separate camps were killed in attacks on the same night in Glacier National Park in Montana in 1967. There have also been deaths from polar bears in the Arctic.

Victims have ranged in age from toddlers to senior citizens. Bears acted with predatory intent or were motivated by protecting their young.

Yellowstone National Park is a place where tourists come to see bears in their natural habitat, but the unpredictable nature of bear behavior is an enduring given.

Wolves are the most elusive of animals inside Yellowstone National Park. Some rescued and captive wolves reside in the Grizzly & Wolf Discovery Center in West Yellowstone, Montana, at the park's West Entrance.

CHAPTER 9
Wolves Exterminated

Starting with the big bad wolf of fairy tales, wolves often have been portrayed as animals of evil intent and a negative presence in stories, the woods, the forest, and roaming the land. Their howl is both mesmerizing and chilling. And in the minds of many, wolves are simply bloodthirsty killers.

That has been a longstanding image and resulted in some devastating policies that affected the population of the big-toothed, dog-like animals that just like other wildlife are simply trying to survive in the wilderness.

From the perspective of one hundred fifty years of Yellowstone National Park, gray wolf policy in the park can be reviewed as confusing, misguided, vicious, altruistic, and an example of mankind tampering with nature.

Wolves are creatures engulfed in mythology, usually inserted into a story as bad guys with no conscience, characterized by selfishness and ruthlessness. In the 1800s, when mountain men first investigated Yellowstone territory, wolves were fair game for their pelts. Settlers who followed and established ranches and farms had no truck with wolves, a species that was prone to mess with their cattle and other livestock.

Government authorities felt citizens putting down roots, establishing farms, and building cities all were measurably more important than the continuation of the wolf as a healthy, respected species in the Greater Yellowstone Ecosystem. There was a shrug if they were a casualty of progress, eliciting little sympathy. At its worst, government policy was malevolent, supported by a general belief that the wolf was at the root of much destruction to the landscape.

Inside the park itself, wolves came to be seen as killers of other animals that tourists wanted to view, particularly elk, and they developed a reputation as the enemy. The only good wolf was a dead wolf, and through poisoning and other methods of killing Yellowstone officials participated in the concerted effort to eradicate wolves in the park. This focus on wiping out the wolf in Yellowstone was at its peak from 1914 to 1926, and by the height of the Roaring Twenties the howling animals had essentially been eliminated in Yellowstone. Every wolf pack authorities were aware of had been tracked down and eradicated, a total of 136 wolves in all during that dozen-year period. Whatever wolves remained were stragglers, solo animals savvy enough to escape with their lives and to stay hidden, so officials could pretend they did not exist at all.

The wolf was essentially a removed species in Yellowstone, though very periodically a sighting was reported to rangers. It was concluded any such wolf spotted in Yellowstone, though, was merely passing through, not a resident wolf. The same pattern was followed throughout most of the Lower 48 states, and few gray wolves remained at large in their natural habitat.

Much like the recognition of the harm done to the bison, after years passed scientists realized wolf eradication had not been a very good idea and had thrown the ecosystem out of balance. A change in philosophy starting in the 1960s bearing upon the composition of wildlife inside Yellowstone led to the conclusion that wolves belonged in the ecosystem and the park. This was also the time officials began to realize they had to rid the park of the garbage dumps that fed the bears.

It was decided wildlife basically should regulate itself. Some authorities began thinking, "Gee, it would be nice if we had wolves here."

However, there was no known breeding pair living in Yellowstone at the time. There was a growing environmental consciousness in the United States, though, and in 1973, Congress approved the Endangered Species Act.

The act directed the US Fish and Wildlife Service to attempt to restore threatened species that were on the brink of elimination. This was a complete turnaround from the policies of the 1920s when man was responsible for putting the gray wolf in jeopardy in the first place. By 1978, the only place in the Lower 48 states (Alaska's wolf population was always abundant) where the wolf was not endangered was Minnesota.

The wolf's status had changed. The federal agency tentatively suggested an experimental group of wolves be returned to Yellowstone to see how it went and what the effects might be on other wildlife. In 1991, Congress appropriated funding for an Environmental Impact Statement and the idea was floated to the American people for comment in 1994. Some 160,000 responses were received and it was decided wolves should be restored to the landscape in Yellowstone.

This was controversial from the start among ranchers who owned property in Montana and Wyoming along the park's borders. They opposed the reintroduction of a predator to the mix that would surely attack and kill cattle, costing them money.

Years of talking and pondering passed before a restoration plan was approved, a plan which also included reintroducing gray wolves to portions of Idaho. The United States cut a deal with Canadian authorities to obtain wolves, and over parts of 1995 and 1996 officials set free thirty-one transplanted gray wolves in Yellowstone and tracked them with radio collars.

Those wolves were probably the most intensively studied animals in the world as scientists eagerly monitored behavior and desperately hoped to learn what effect a fresh top-of-the-food-chain

Scientists study wolves in the field in the 2000s after their reintroduction to Yellowstone National Park. (Credit: US Fish and Wildlife Service)

predator would have on other animals in the park. Radio collars have been an invaluable tool, and the reintroduced wolves and their generational successors have had virtually no privacy. Wherever they go, even if invisible from the eye along the park road, they are still tracked through electronics.

Wolves, as the phrase goes and has morphed into a cliché, do travel in packs. Packs consist of a manageable ten or so animals, and there is a hierarchy within the group with alpha males and alpha females. When it comes to stalking, or the hunt, they work in concert. Wolves on the prowl for food tend to gravitate toward a weaker member of an elk, deer, or buffalo herd, the older or infirm, looking for the animal easy to separate out from the protective umbrella of the group. The wolves work as a team to bring down the prey, then kill and devour it. Wolves do like meat more than vegetables, and in winter it is gauged that 90 percent of their winter diet can be elk meat, meaning they take a toll on the elk population, especially elk that did not prepare well for the cold and stormy season and are weaker.

By no means are all wolves friendly toward one another. The groups have their own turf and defend it against intruders, including other wolf packs. There is no share and share alike between gangs.

People who view wolf videos, watching them hunt together and then tear apart apparently bigger and stronger animals, do wonder about their own futures as they wander around in the wild if they were to stumble on a pack. It is wise to take precautions, although most often wolves melt away into the woods or the darkness rather than seek human interaction.

By 2002, wolves were established in Yellowstone, or, it should be said, re-established. The public was gaga over them. They were almost like a new attraction at Disneyland, something novel to see and experience. One thing about wolves, however, especially compared to bison, elk, deer, and even bears, is that they are much more reclusive. Park officials suggest the best chance of seeing a wolf in Yellowstone is at either dawn or dusk when they tend to move around the most.

That doesn't mean they frequent the park roads. Unless they are hunting for food, wolves tend to stay in the backcountry. Except for ranchers worried about their cattle, the average Yellowstone visitor ranked seeing a wolf high on their to-do list when visiting the park. Whether they got to see one or not depended on their luck and dedication.

In order to spy a wolf a tourist should be supplied with high-powered binoculars, a telescope, or a super powerful photographic lens. Professional photographers who make a career out of selling pictures of wolves have to be blessed with extraordinary patience. There are selected turnoffs near the highway running through the park where the pros gathered, carrying lenses that seemed so large the shooters might have to be on a weight-lifting program to carry them. These photographers waited and waited for select wolf packs to show themselves at certain times of the day in hopes of obtaining a fantastic image magazine editors would drool over. It is

One of the wolves that lives at the Grizzly & Wolf Discovery Center in West Yellowstone, Montana.

Douglas W. Smith was the wildlife biologist in Yellowstone who oversaw the reintroduction of the gray wolf in the park in the 1990s and still works with the wolf packs today.

a time-consuming method, and the wolves must be cooperative at the right time.

Wolves are larger than most dogs but may not be as large as many people think. The average weight of a male wolf is one hundred ten pounds, and they reach one hundred thirty pounds. The average weight of the adult female is ninety pounds.

Unlike many domestic dogs, though, the lifespan of a Yellowstone wolf is not terribly lengthy. The average life lasts just under five years. It can be a tough existence foraging for every meal, providing for a pack, and putting up with extreme winter weather. Scientists estimate that 77 percent of the wolves that perish inside Yellowstone die of natural causes. But many wolves in the Greater Yellowstone Ecosystem do die from human-related causes. That could be as simple as being hit by a car, but there are also wolf hunting seasons in the surrounding states where the animals can be harvested in certain numbers set each year.

There are regulated hunting seasons in place in Wyoming, Montana, and Idaho that enable hunters to kill wolves within certain regions. Those areas do border Yellowstone, and if a wolf strays into those states from the park at the wrong time of year, it can legally be taken.

How this can impact Yellowstone wolves, who can't read road signs, was illustrated anew in January 2022. Montana wildlife commissioners, who are not necessarily regarded as the wolves' best friends, abruptly shut down the gray wolf hunting season adjacent to Yellowstone because they were under siege by critics. Complaints stockpiled due to an unusual spate of wolf hunting, shooting, trapping, and the like resulting in the deaths of twenty-three wolves that had crossed the park boundary.

More than twenty-five years have passed since the wolf reintroduction program began in Yellowstone, and this was the largest diminishment of Yellowstone wolves through hunting in any single year. The population was beefed up by the restoration program, but the original wolves have long ago passed away. Despite the restoration, it is not as if Yellowstone is overrun by thousands of wolves—nor is that true across the United States. Of the approximately sixty-seven thousand gray wolves in North America, fifty-three thousand of them reside in Canada.

There was quite a hullabaloo when the first trucks rolled into Yellowstone National Park with a cargo of wolf transplants from Canada those many years ago, each of which was radio collared by the time it was released and more or less became its own science project.

One thing park officials did was avoid naming the wolves. They did not want to

Douglas W. Smith, who has spent the last quarter century studying the wolves of Yellowstone, in the field with a gray wolf. (Credit: US Fish and Wildlife Service)

anthropomorphize them, something wolf fans were all too willing to do. In some instances people bestowed names on select wolves anyway, but wolves respond to the call of the wild, not the call of their names. Rangers and scientists stuck with a numbering system for referring to specific wolves. It was efficient and not sentimental.

One aspect that stands out relating to the wolf restoration project is continuity. Biologist Dr. Douglas W. Smith has been involved from the start. He was on the scene when wolves were released. In 2002, a visitor could approach him in his Yellowstone office to obtain tips on where and how to see a wolf in the flesh. In 2019 he was still touring the area on demand, speaking in places like nearby Cody, Wyoming, near the East Entrance of the park, repeating the story of the wolves' reintroduction and the steady monitoring over the intervening years keeping track of the current packs and studying the species' behavior.

To a large extent, Smith, who previously worked with wolves at Isle Royale National Park in Michigan, and also in Minnesota, has made wolves and their link to Yellowstone his life's work.

"Our goal is to protect them," Smith said. Even if adjacent states' hunting and regulatory laws sometimes seem to conspire against that.

In 1995, the restoration was named the Yellowstone Wolf Project, and it still bears that name. Annual reports are produced, and Smith is still in the thick of the wolf world inside the park. A quarter of a century after the first wolves returned to Yellowstone by way of Canada, Smith is still around to offer the answers to everyone's questions. The wolf, a century ago a species destroyed in the park, now lives life quite differently in Yellowstone. The wolves are free to roam, though like any pedestrian, they must look both ways before crossing the street—if that street leads beyond Yellowstone's borders.

This radio-collared wolf in Yellowstone weighed in at one hundred thirty pounds. (Credit: US Fish and Wildlife Service)

For such a large lake, with one hundred ten miles of shoreline, Yellowstone Lake regularly freezes in winter and is slow to thaw in spring.

CHAPTER 10
Yellowstone Lake

Yellowstone Lake seemed so vast when first glimpsed by humans that one might confuse it with a third ocean. As it was, Captain William Clark mentioned it in his journal on the Corps of Discovery trip (the members did see some of Yellowstone's special places, even if they did not linger to check them out in more detail), and mountain man John Colter reported to outsiders that this territory contained such a huge body of water, those skeptics were already dismissing claims of the other wonders of the Yellowstone area.

The lake is not an ocean, but it is massive and impressive, as are so many other aspects of Yellowstone National Park. Standing along one shore, the visitor cannot see the other side, or sides, given the manner in which the shoreline winds. On a windy day, water will churn and waves roll, waves that do not seem inviting to the boater. Often enough, there are bumpy conditions readily felt on the surface.

Yet the lake is very much one of the cornerstone natural features of the vast park. Yellowstone is home to numerous bodies of water: smaller lakes, streams, creeks, sloughs, and rivers, including the winding, lengthy Yellowstone River, a haven for trout anglers. But Yellowstone Lake is the heart of the park away from land, an enticing, visual glory that begs tourists to come aboard and try it out on a tour boat or a fishing boat.

In dimensions, Yellowstone Lake is sizable. Its location alone sometimes gives pause, because it is situated at 7,732 feet of altitude. This is the largest freshwater lake higher than seven thousand feet in North America. An offshoot of that position is the freezing of the lake in a place that experiences long and harsh winters. Regularly, the water freezes to a depth of three feet, although in some areas, where the lake is close to hot springs, the temperature emanating from the boiling water and steam prevents the freeze-over.

Yellowstone Lake is 136 square miles, most definitely separating it from ponds. It features 110 miles of shoreline. This means when the modern-day automobile driver follows park roads, the lake is in sight for many miles. Occasionally, it dips out of view, blocked by the trees, but then it abruptly appears again many miles down the highway. This can give the impression that the visitor is gazing upon a different body of water when in reality it is just another corner of Yellowstone Lake.

At its deepest point, Yellowstone Lake has a depth of 394 feet, although from shore to shore the average depth is 139 feet.

Native Americans who hunted and lived in the region were well aware of Yellowstone Lake and its attributes thousands of years before the first White settlers came to the area. From Colter on, mountain men hunted and trapped in the vicinity, and although their markets were to the east and they did not build cabins or homes near the lake, they too were quite aware of the significant body of water. Some of them recorded their impressions upon first seeing the lake; the size particularly grabbed their attention against a backdrop of low-slung mountains.

Just as they did when touring the area's forests and noting its wildlife, the early government expeditions took pains to draft their own accounts about the lake. In some of those reports, the variety of wildlife that hovered in the area was said to include thousands of waterfowl and plentiful supplies of fish, especially what came to be called Yellowstone cutthroat trout, the lake's prized species.

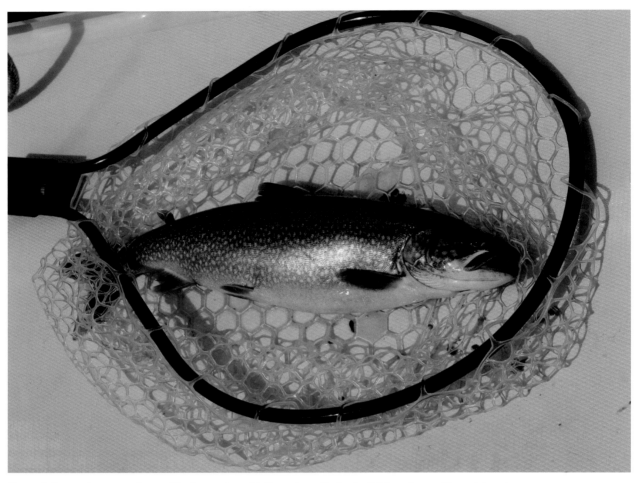

One of the main attractions of being out on Yellowstone Lake is fishing for cutthroat trout.

None of the exploratory parties set out on the mission to specifically circle or map the entirety of the lake. Each described segments from limited viewpoints, though the overall message was that Yellowstone (originally called Yellow Stone by Clark) was a huge lake teeming with wildlife and waterfowl activity.

Lieutenant Gustavus C. Doane with the Washburn Expedition described some of what that group saw and experienced. His imagination was taken by distant islands, which he felt were begging to be explored.

These islands doubtless have never been trodden by human footsteps and still belong to the regions of the unexplored. We built a raft for the purpose of attempting to visit them, but the strong waves of the lake dashed it to pieces in an hour.

Numerous steam jets pour out from the bluffs on the shore at different points. The waters of the lake reflect a deep blue color, are clear as crystal, and doubtless of great depth near the center. The extreme elevation of this great body of water [Doane called it 7,714 3/5 feet] is difficult to realize. Place Mount Washington, the pride of New England, with its base at the sea level, at the bottom of the lake, and the clear waters of the latter would roll 2,214 feet above its summit. With the single exception of Lake Titicaca, Peru, it is the highest great body of water on the globe.

That observation was incorrect, but Yellowstone's elevation is still notable.

The artist Thomas Moran, on one of those early expeditions, also recognized the singular beauty of Yellowstone Lake as a potential canvas for painters.

Despite its beauty and stature, at various times (primarily between 1920 and 1937) politicians sought to dam the lake, always with some so-called public benefit project at the bottom of the scheme. All proposals were defeated.

From a recreational standpoint, there has been an interest in boating almost from the moment when Yellowstone became a park. While there was little management supervision during those years, the early tourists went back to the days of the Nez Percé hostilities.

It was in 1890 when the first boating permits on Yellowstone Lake were granted to the Yellowstone Boat Company. The boats were for functional use, as part of transportation, not for tours. They were used to ferry people between roads on different sides of the lake. Most of the visitors were traveling by stagecoach and were practically choked by dust kicked up on the dirt roads. Any time spent on the water enjoying a breeze would have been a respite.

"I think it would have been very refreshing," said modern-day interpretive ranger Tom Vanzant, who provides lectures to visitors who take boat rides for fun on Yellowstone Lake.

In the 1890s, however, an era in which steamships sailed upon the Great Lakes in the Midwest, someone suggested steamship rides on Yellowstone Lake.

As had been the case from the very beginning

For well over a century, Yellowstone National Park has offered boat tours on Yellowstone Lake to visitors, these days on vessels like this one.

of Yellowstone's time as a national park, there were some entrepreneurs who sought to make money off its existence and appeal to tourists. The man who did so from a boating standpoint was the aptly named E. C. Waters. He backed the steamship-on-the-lake tours and obtained a permit to run a business.

After a search for what he deemed an appropriate boat for his venture, Waters dismantled a boat into sections and managed to transport it from Lake Minnetonka in Minnesota to Yellowstone Lake in 1889. Waters's vessel was called the *Zillah*. It was a bit of an overused boat that might have had a capacity of one hundred twenty for a tour but did not have a solid reputation for seaworthiness.

For all its shaky past history, the *Zillah* proved a success. Waters's rides received good reviews, although Waters himself did not. He made enemies more readily than friends. He seemed to be a guy who spent more effort looking for trouble than the easy way to get along, and he tangled with his benefactors inside the park and at the Department of the Interior. This did not bode well for a long-term future business relationship.

Waters, though, saw himself as a visionary. He figured since the *Zillah* had worked out, he could expand his on-lake efforts with a newer and bigger boat. He invested in a second boat that was one hundred twenty-five feet long and could transport six hundred passengers at a time. The man named the boat after himself, the *E. C. Waters*, and in 1905 he enthusiastically approached the opportunity to offer many more rides. The boat was not ready by the tourist season, but Waters arranged for a christening ceremony anyway with a keynote speaker, F. D. Geiger, editor of the nearby Gardiner, Montana, newspaper.

"For sixteen years, the *Zillah* freighted with human souls has made her trips to and from the thumb of the lake to the Lake Hotel," Geiger said. "She has carried the rich and the poor, the old and the young, the great people and the Smiths,

and never has one of her passengers needed a life preserver or a bathing suit."

In his newspaper, *The Wonderland*, Geiger called the new ship "the Pride of Yellowstone Lake" and predicted Waters, the man, would be remembered by history as "one of the West's great promoters." Instead, though it was too soon to know at that moment, he was soon to be almost completely forgotten.

The boat christening was a chance, a day, for Waters to feel good about the future. But a deep level of melancholy was taking hold in him because his teenaged daughter had committed suicide.

Also, things from a business standpoint deteriorated right when they should have been looking good. Waters's feuds with the government cost him. Officials refused to grant him a renewal on his business permit. Outraged and prone to conflict, Waters went to war over the waters. Bitter and loud about it, Waters was soon labeled "the most hated man in Yellowstone."

In 1907, Waters was banned from Yellowstone, exiled in writing by the then-superintendent

One great fear amongst fisheries experts in the park is the possibility of invasive species such as zebra mussels infecting waterways. A possible remedy is use of trained dogs to sniff them out.

Samuel B. M. Young. The strongly worded order read in part, "E. C. Waters, president of the Yellowstone Lake Boat Company, having rendered himself obnoxious is . . . debarred from the park." He was not to be allowed back within Yellowstone's boundaries without the written permission of secretary of the interior or the park superintendent.

After two decades as a fixture at the lake, Waters was out. He wanted to sell his business for $300,000, boats included. Before Waters could receive an offer (though it was not certain if conditions could be met anyway because of the government's blockage of the permit), the government cut a deal with another company to become the lake's tour-boat operator.

Meanwhile, the boat *E. C. Waters* sat paralyzed at a cove near uninhabited Stevenson Island, unable to make tours. Waters left his new boat to rot, and the boat never carried paying customers. Then, in 1921, massive winds came up and blew the *E. C. Waters* free of its moorings and across the water a short distance onto the sand at Stevenson Island.

The boat beached itself and remained there. Later, a salvage operation took the boiler from the ship and installed it at the Lake Hotel. It provided heat to the hotel for forty-six years while a few miles away the shell of the ship foundered. It remained in view of other boat riders, though. For kicks, partygoers sailed out to the wreck and held soirees on the site.

Annoyed by what they considered an eyesore, in 1931, a group of park rangers on a clean-up mission in 1931 made an on-site call to burn the *E. C. Waters* to ash. The attempt failed, and when word got back to tour boat operators, who loved talking about the backstory of the wreck, such future efforts were forbidden.

In the early 2020s, the hulk of the boat could still be seen in the water. In a sense, the *E. C. Waters* had become the *Titanic* of Yellowstone Lake.

While people don't swim in Yellowstone Lake because of cold water temperatures, waterfowl enjoy the experience.

E. C. Waters, the person, died in 1926. He would probably be somewhat amused to know that his prized passenger boat is not only still present on Yellowstone Lake, albeit in dilapidated form, but is also regularly referred to by interpretive rangers on the lake telling his and the boat's story to new generations of tourists while they take their own rides on smaller and less luxurious boats.

Anglers come from all over the United States to say they have gone fly fishing in Yellowstone National Park.

CHAPTER 11
Yellowstone Fishing

In the early days, fishing was about subsistence, not sport angling. Catch a fish, eat a fish. That's how Native Americans operated. They did not mount the skins on the walls of the teepees as souvenirs.

As the park modernized, stabilized, became more civilized in the sense the visitors were tourists, not Native Americans or White mountain men who wanted to live off the land, fishing for fun became one of the grandest of attractions.

Rivers and lakes wooed visitors enthralled by the swirling waters, enticed by the fish living beneath the waves in Yellowstone Lake and in the rivers—the Yellowstone, the Madison, the Firehole, the Gibbon, and the Gallatin—where fly fishermen congregate.

When Yellowstone was barely a teenager, anglers learned about the remarkable fishing opportunities within its boundaries because of the staple outdoor magazines that played upon the fantasies of those who could afford to travel. There were always big fish beyond the next mountain, in the West of the imagination.

Sports Afield was founded in 1887, *Field and Stream* in 1895, and *Outdoor Life* in 1898. It seemed mandatory for someone connected to those magazines to write about the fishing in Yellowstone. Fishermen willing to take a train could venture to the park for a wilderness experience unlike what was available near their homes. They didn't have to board a steamship to a distant land or get out on the ocean.

"They made the fisheries popular in the East," said Todd Koel, who in recent years has been the supervising biologist of fisheries in Yellowstone for the National Park Service. "For sure, when the park was created, people were fishing right away."

Some of the earliest expeditions surveying Yellowstone before it became a park—the Washburn and Hayden groups—fished, but did so for food during their stays.

Long before there was even a park service, though some years after the odd superintendent term of Nathaniel Langford, government supervisors began stocking fish in bodies of water within Yellowstone. The first stocking program began in 1889. However, science was not so wise or concerned with what species of fish were dropped off. Even if various kinds of trout are prized by anglers in many parts of the world, brook trout and rainbow trout were not native to this area. People like brook trout and rainbow trout, but purists are retroactively dismayed that those fish were introduced to Yellowstone.

An agency called the United States Fish Commission was established in 1871 and was assigned the job of promoting fishing around the country. In Yellowstone, individuals were encouraged to fish for the adventure of it, standing beside or floating upon pristine waters against a backdrop of snow-covered mountains.

Another publication (which did not have the staying power of the big three magazines, which are still at least digitally readable today) was called *Outing: Sport, Adventure, Travel, Fiction*. In 1897 that magazine carried a story headlined "A Woman's Trout-Fishing in Yellowstone Park." The author, Mary Trowbridge Townsend, was not favorably impressed with fish in Yellowstone Lake at first. "Fishing in the Yellowstone region has long been looked upon with disfavor by all true lovers of angling," she said. "They remember the Lake with its cannibal myriads of ghoul-like fish—I can hardly call them trout—big-headed, with thin, parasite-covered bodies, so starved, so eager to escape the horrors of their struggle for existence that they rush madly at the fly, thankful for the chance to die."

Certainly a mixed review, although those sentences did make it sound as if it was easy to catch a fish.

Townsend felt much differently about the trout swimming in the rivers; she said it was a thrill to catch one of those fish. Bringing in one of the trout after a serious battle was more satisfying. She wrote, "Long dashes downstream taxed any unsteady footing. The sharp click and whir of the reel resounded in desperate efforts to hold him back somewhat in check." Presumably, Townsend thought this was a prettier fish.

Yellowstone proved experimental ground for the stocking of different types of fish, many of which did not thrive or really belong in the climate or setting and, one way or another, through their own demise or human removal, eventually disappeared. Those ranged from largemouth bass to Atlantic salmon and yellow perch.

Alaskan Alison Willis took a family fishing trip on Yellowstone Lake.

The cutthroat trout is native to Yellowstone, however. It was the most popular and prized fish anglers sought. The colorful, speckled fish, streaked with yellowish-brown skin and a reddish slash along the jaw, is a member of the salmon family and is native to only a few states in the West. Yellowstone Lake and the Yellowstone River contain the largest population of cutthroat in the world, making them a very desirable species for visitors. Clear, cold water is the main habitat of the cutthroat trout.

Although Yellowstone's dominant fish from its inception as a national park, cutthroat trout proved too popular over the decades and could have been completely fished out if not for the aid of the National Park Service and its policies. The population had plummeted after years of fishing. Even more threatening, in 2007, it was discovered that a voracious invasive species, lake trout, was swiftly gobbling up cutthroat in Yellowstone Lake and might well wipe out the cornerstone species without drastic action.

Long before, the importance of cutthroat trout to the Yellowstone environment was recognized by the US Fish Commission. Between 1889 and 1996, some 310 million fish were stocked in the park.

Despite those long-term efforts, officials realized brown trout and rainbow trout were taking over the creeks and streams and pushing cutthroat out. This was a serious blow to the ecology and future of the park. Between sixteen and twenty species of birds and animals rely on cutthroat trout as part of their diets. This includes the alpha animal, the grizzly bear, which sometimes could be seen on the shore pawing for fish.

In the 1950s, years before lake trout became an invasive species issue in the lake, the population of cutthroat was already diminishing steadily. Although early superintendents Stephen Mather and Horace Albright probably could not fathom such a description, their park had become too popular. At least in the sense of hosting too many fishermen, all of whom wanted to catch and keep cutthroat.

Beginning in 1902, and for decades, one

Yellowstone landmark that was a must-visit for everyone was Fishing Bridge. And if you were an angler, that also meant you had to stop at the (initially log, concrete from 1937 on) bridge spanning a narrow section of the Yellowstone River, whip out rod and reel, lean over the side, and catch fish.

What was a ritual led to matters getting out of hand. Anglers crowded onto the bridge, elbowing one another out of position, and threw out a line. Others paddled up to the bridge in canoes and fished below. This was like catching fish in a barrel. The fish stood little chance, and their long-term future was being harmed.

Eventually, the National Park Service took control of the situation. Although cutthroat trout still gather at the bridge to spawn, fishing has been halted. Those who climb out of their

The most serious anglers who visit Yellowstone prefer to fish for trout on the rivers, such as the Madison, Lamar, Yellowstone, or Firehole.

automobiles at Fishing Bridge nowadays and walk out onto the bridge do so to watch the fish swim around. Look, but don't touch.

While there would be some symmetry to a day in the future when Fishing Bridge could once more be a focal point of fishing, such a move is not in the immediate park plans, or any long-term ones, either. Ironically, Fishing Bridge was reconstructed in 2020, though for the benefit of motorists.

"Oh, no, I'd say never," Koel said of the likelihood of resumed fishing at Fishing Bridge. "It has evolved into a fish viewing spot."

One day the Yellowstone Lake water temperature was at fifty degrees Fahrenheit, pretty much ideal for the fish, though too cold to entertain the notion of swimming. And anglers riding along in boats definitely didn't want to fall in. There are times the lake can produce six-foot waves, making it seem as gnarly as an ocean, or almost an invitation for the surfing minded.

As has been for well more than a century, Yellowstone National Park overall remains a fishing destination for anglers from afar. If the fisherman is a cutthroat aficionado, there really is nowhere else to go in his mind. He must return to Yellowstone, just as salmon do to original homes to spawn.

From the days of the free-for-all, when a fish caught meant a dead fish, to a more progressive catch-and-release outlook that has ingrained itself in the minds of many, especially fly fishermen, the cutthroat remains a desired species. Where once it was about taking the fish home for many meals, now the philosophy seems more focused on the sport of it all, the desire for the fight, to bring in the fish, but then set it free. For many, the act of fishing has certainly superseded the act of catching and keeping.

Yellowstone regulations are now all about preserving the future of the species, even while allowing for the pleasure of fishing within the park. For many, Yellowstone National Park is a pilgrimage destination. Being permitted to fish for cutthroat on the spectacular Yellowstone Lake or the legendary Yellowstone River is personal tradition for many.

Sometimes that proud tradition and heritage is in the blood of people who live right down the road from the park. One such angler is Bob Devine, who lives in West Yellowstone, Montana, the community that abuts the park where the West Entrance is located. He loves trout fishing so much he enters the park to cast four or five times a week in summer.

"It's my favorite place," Devine said. "It's so scenic here. There aren't many fish, but there are big ones." Under Devine's definition "big ones" are twenty inches long or more.

Husband and wife Walter Gerlesky and Jane Massey of Franklin, New Jersey, were encountered on the Yellowstone River one summer that happened to be their fifteenth July fly fishing in the park. Gerlesky taught Massey how to fly fish on one of those trips in Yellowstone made expressly to visit cutthroat. They have become friends with other couples from around the country who make the same July sojourn each year.

"They're the ultimate," Gerlesky said of cutthroat trout. One time, Gerlesky said, he and Massey caught twelve fish in a single spot. That was a trip to remember.

There are different fishing dates for Yellowstone Lake and for Yellowstone's rivers. Since the park is located at six thousand-plus feet of elevation and higher, in Wyoming, Montana (and a sliver of Idaho), the lakes do not thaw out for fishing very early in spring. Depending on the area of the park, it could snow where people like to fish.

For many, however, annual opening day on the rivers is a ritual, a tradition, a personal holiday of sorts. When fishing begins for the season in Yellowstone, they want to be part of it. Many of those who live nearby year-round choose to put X marks on their personal calendars to be present for the season opener. Fishing is allowed beginning on the Saturday of Memorial Day weekend.

Robert Metzger, who was seventy years old in summer 2019, had been coming to Yellowstone from Seattle to fish since 1958. When he retired from the professional world, he moved to

Much of the fishing in the park is catch and release.

Montana to be much closer to Yellowstone. "I had to be here on opening day," Metzger said.

He was hardly alone in feeling the urge to be present on some river in Yellowstone when the starting gun sounded. Pam Parker drove to the Firehole River from Idaho to stand in her waders as the river ran through her. She was reminded that fishing does not guarantee catching when she put in a steady half-hour of casting before she felt a nibble.

Her first fish of the day was hardly larger than a goldfish, but it was a fish and it counted, even if it was swiftly released and Parker's attention turned back to increasing the haul load.

"A tiny one," she said of the first catch. "I was looking for its dad." A reasonable thought since the trout she set free was barely five inches long.

Parker did not come to Yellowstone on this trip expecting to hook a passel of fish, but she hoped for the best and reveled in being outdoors with a rod in her hands in an environment that made her heart sing.

"It's kind of a special day for fishermen," Parker said of clocking in on opening day. "I love Yellowstone."

Operator of a fishing gear shop and a guide service in Cody, Wyoming, Tim Wade is one of the longtime experts in Yellowstone fishing. He remembers when the catch was bigger, there were more fish, and the cutthroat were not threatened. He has been coming to Yellowstone for the opener almost without interruption since 1982, though once in a while he appeared at a different time on opening weekend.

"You see people from all over the world," Wade said.

Wade laments the hardships visited upon cutthroat and said until about 2000 an angler putting in a full day might catch between seventy-five and one hundred fish on the opening day. He said "the fish were dumb." By that, Wade meant, it had been seven months since the trout had come across a hook and they seemed to have forgotten what an issue that posed. Now there were just fewer fish to be caught.

Another old-timer, who at one point had a twenty-five-year streak of participating in openers, was George Simonton, another Cody, Wyoming, angler. Simonton's habit was to drive a camper into the park the day before the opener and then rise early to get a jump on the fish the first day it was permissible to throw out a line. Simonton said he had hooked fifty to seventy-five fish in a day, and one year caught ten to fifteen fish in a two-hour period without moving from a spot and while casting to the same log.

One opening day, Yellowstone pretty much

Opening day of fishing on rivers in Yellowstone has become a tradition for many anglers.

proving its point about weather, Simonton said he got caught in a twelve-inch snowstorm. Remember, that was around Memorial Day.

Another time, he said, he was sitting around a bar in West Yellowstone after a full day of fishing the opener and ended up talking with a couple from New York. They had driven straight through to Montana in anticipation of the opener and then rested a whole day on the sidelines. By accident. They thought the opener was Sunday, not Saturday, so they missed it. Oops. "Sorry, pal," is what Simonton said upon hearing this tale.

Parker continued fishing on the Firehole River. She moved around, wading into deeper water, retreating closer to shore. She cast from a new spot and entangled a fly in a nearby tree. This one was going to have to be catch and release. No chainsaws allowed to retrieve the fishing gear. The flip side of the matter, though, some joked, was that Yellowstone National Park regulations say there is a one-tree limit.

Elk don't mind spending time with their friends. In rutting season, however, one take-charge bull might try to keep many females around him.

CHAPTER 12

Elk

The giant male elk stood proud and solitary, chest deep in the Madison River, not far from where a Yellowstone road ran out of the park into West Yellowstone, Montana.

It was the fall rutting season and this big guy was the king of the neighborhood, the ruler of a harem of several other female elk who stuck around with him. When the mood struck him he bugled, and the air was penetrated by his loud voice.

His antler rack was tall and well-formed, six tines on a side, giving the mighty male an aura of power and invincibility. No other male was horning in on his territory.

Males can grow to be seven hundred pounds, very muscular and sturdy animals. Female adults, or cows, may weigh five hundred pounds. When babies are born, they tend to weigh in the thirty-pound range. After the September–October rut, when the males lose their minds over female companionship, calves are born in May or June of the following year.

Elk spend much of their energy and feeding efforts focused on grass varieties, sedge, and herbs and consider the bark of aspen trees to be tasty treats. They are basically vegetarians that devour the bark of burned trees and conifer needles. They are not meat eaters, but unfortunately for them, they may well become the meat dish for powerful enemies inside the park.

Elk are among the most popularly viewed wildlife in Yellowstone. Sightings are not as coveted as driving up alongside a grizzly bear, black bear, or a wolf, but elk are far more numerous. The size of the Yellowstone elk herds in summer can reach between ten thousand and twenty thousand head. They are divided into smaller herds and roam throughout the 2.2 million acres of parkland. They may often be seen alongside the road, unpredictably so, but not in numbers bunched as tightly together or as numerous as bison.

There are more elk by far than bears and wolves combined inside Yellowstone. They are members of the deer family, and in Shawnee, one local Native American tongue, they are referred to as *wapiti*. There is a small community named Wapiti on the outskirts of Cody, Wyoming, which tourists pass through on the drive to the East Entrance of Yellowstone. Wapiti is one place where William F. "Buffalo Bill" Cody, who died in 1917, built a hotel to capture tourist clientele headed to Yellowstone. The word *wapiti* actually means white deer in Shawnee, though elk's coats are more brownish, with a hint of redness. That accounts for the European name of red deer for the same animal.

In an intriguing language muck-up, elk is the word for moose in parts of Europe, so European tourists are often fooled by conversations that refer to elk herds in the United States. The number of moose within Yellowstone and its environs is very limited.

The elk don't block cars in the roads, but they can offer surprise viewing for photographers and the curious by occasionally congregating in groups of fifteen or twenty at a time in grassy areas not far off Grand Loop Road. They pause and forage for greens for hours at a time in places where the visitor can obtain pictures or scenes that are completely unobstructed by trees.

It is never advisable to wander too close to an elk, but they will mostly leave humans alone if they are not hassled or do not feel their young are in jeopardy. An aggressive mother who feels a threat, however, is an aggressive mama in any language.

Elk are among the comparatively tamer of the large species of animals in Yellowstone. Often, numerous elk hang out at Mammoth Hot Springs, reclining on the lawns around the hotel and concessions buildings.

Elk have it good in the warmer summer months, with plenty of food to eat, plenty of area to roam around. But winter is another matter altogether. The harshness of negative-forty-degree temperatures with violent winds, ice storms, and major snowstorms represent a killing season for elk. It is easy for the animals to starve. Weaker members of the herds, due to age, illness, hunger, or other weakness, become easy prey in late fall for bears stockpiling calories for winter hibernation or for wolves. The same can be true in early spring when the park comes alive again. Elk that barely made it through the winter are targeted by emerging bears and aggressive wolves.

Sometimes those elk die on their own, and bears and wolves feed on their carcasses. Both of those species become quite protective of gut piles and dead meat, on the lookout for one another sneaking in to steal a previously deceased elk.

Thousands of elk may die during the off-season. Also, during the winter, elk tend to breach the boundaries of Yellowstone and drift to places where the quality of the plant life is more reliable, reducing the park population to four thousand during the dark and cold of winter.

For many, visiting Yellowstone is like dropping in on a wild outdoor preserve, akin in their minds to a wilderness preserve. While hunting these elk inside the park is illegal, there is elk hunting permitted as a popular pastime not only elsewhere in the West, but also in nearby states.

The whitetail deer has proliferated throughout much of the United States. Elk only live and thrive in selected states. A person who spends enough time hanging out in Colorado is bound to bump into elk. That state is home to 280,000 elk. The elk may not be renowned for their size in that state, but they certainly fit the description of being abundant.

There are numerous other states where there is some elk hunting regulated by state departments of natural resources. That includes Wyoming, where the elk may trot between state lines and park lines and possibly be hunted if they are in the wrong place at the wrong time. Elk are prime species for bow or gun hunters in the early autumn when the animals are at the peak of their fitness and are hot after the females of the species. Their bugling is basically an announcement to the girls that they are ready, willing, and able to mate and that they are worthy specimens.

Bugling may also signal a readiness for a fight with another full-fledged male elk over territory and in gaining domination over a mating target, somewhat like a bar fight between two slightly addled human males. A few years ago, two full-sized, rowdy elk, very much engaged in what they were doing and what they were after, put on a show for tourists at Mammoth Hot Springs, wielding antlers in battle for a long time without resolution of who was the genuine king of the castle. As the elk came at one another and retreated, they led with their antlers, which made a clacking sound as they struck one another. On contact, the elk issued grunts from deep inside the chest, either expressions of their will and energy, or a signal they were tiring from the fight.

Including the entire Greater Yellowstone Ecosystem, there may be thirty thousand to forty thousand elk in the region, not all protected by the rules of Yellowstone National Park, and possibly subject to local hunting governance, depending

For the most part elk will offer a magnificent pose for the amateur photographer, though visitors are discouraged from getting too close and sparking a rare temper display.

This elk is soaking up some sunshine at Mammoth Hot Springs.

on the time of year and location. The Jackson, Wyoming, herd alone has in recent years totaled more than eleven thousand animals, which at a given time would be larger than the Yellowstone National Park herds combined.

When it comes to hunting, elk are prized species because they are large animals, provide a bounty of food from a kill, and are renowned for being lean, healthy, and tasty meat. Hunting magazines or websites online periodically rank the finest elk hunting grounds by polling their readers, who are hunters.

There is also the attraction of hunting elk with prominent antlers for trophy-mounting purposes. That provides dual motivation for the hunter in the field.

No state can match Colorado for its huge population of elk, and most of the best locations are in the West. One exception in these rankings is Pennsylvania, where one writer joked that the state had to be included since it had a geographic area within its borders called Elk County.

Otherwise, such states as Arizona, Washington, New Mexico, Oregon, Utah, Montana, Wyoming, and Idaho are among the most highly rated destinations. It may surprise some that Oregon has more elk than Wyoming and Montana. What is unknown, however, is how the future of the elk herds and populations—and the hunting—will survive the horrendous fires of 2020 in such places as Oregon in particular. Arizona is an unusual case. In 1913, some eighty-three elk were transplanted from Yellowstone and slightly more than a century later the state herd numbers had expanded to between thirty thousand and thirty-five thousand.

As the decade was turning to 2020, it was estimated there were more than one million elk across the United States.

Yellowstone National Park, though, is not about hunting, except if the foolish try to poach an elk, an illegal act that can be severely punished if the perpetrator is caught.

Mostly, elk in Yellowstone are about *oohs* and *ahhs* with travelers from a great distance coming upon small clusters of the animals peacefully munching on veggies and handy enough to have their pictures taken. Perhaps the most reliable place to see elk within the park is in and around Mammoth Hot Springs. This is one of the main gathering spots inside the park for tourists, a crossroads for different directions that also is a central area for food and bathroom breaks and where National Park Service officials live and work.

Over time elk have become peaceful neighbors in the midst of this hubbub, often twenty or thirty at a time spread out on various lawns in the immediate vicinity. No doubt they have learned this is a safe zone. Mostly, females gather and mix here, though nearby there may be a big bull in protective mode. These elk are almost like the pets of the park, but the National Park Service constantly warns visitors not to treat them like pets. Do not feed the elk. Do not walk too close to the elk. Do not approach the elk for close-up photographs.

A few years ago, what seemed like a benign group of elk, regular hangers-on next to buildings such as the Mammoth Hot Springs Hotel,

Now you see me, now you don't. Reclining in tall grass can provide cover.

and usually showing only the mildest of interest in the paths workers followed to their living quarters, initiated conflicts. Twice, elk reared up and attacked workers trying to scurry past, injuring them and sending them to the hospital for medical treatment. It was not obvious what provoked the bad-tempered reactions to people, but the alarm was sounded as a reminder to steer clear of five-hundred-pound animals with hooves that can break bones.

Most of the time, though, if a tourist would like an elk picture, the animals in this area are quite obliging. They trot around, shifting locations, pause to eat some vegetation, lie down on the grass, and nap and kill the day as each group of camera-wielders moves in briefly and snaps shutters.

Oftentimes, there are so many elk creating a commotion for so many hundreds of tourists in this area that the National Park Service stations rangers on the scene to ensure safety for the people and to keep the elk from getting riled up. *Make way, make way*, the rangers sometimes say as an elk wishes to cross the road.

Periodically, elk will roam into the adjacent housing locations near National Park Service offices, pedestrian passersby of a sort, surprising residents when they pause to munch, or show up even a dozen at a time. Such a situation arose in September 2020 when ten or twelve elk decided to visit a house and check out the grass. There were males in the bunch and they were apparently on the prowl for female companionship, letting loose some loud bugling and some screams from deep in the throat. They sounded like show-offs, as in "Look at me!"

While there are always a multitude of elk inside Yellowstone National Park, in winter many thousand participate in a great migration. They drop down from higher elevations, many departing the park, passing through nearby Grand Teton National Park and alighting at the National Elk Refuge in Jackson, Wyoming. Instinctively, the elk know this is the place to be, where they can rest, recline, be fed, and spend months in repose where their biggest responsibility on a given day is to act as a photo opportunity for tourists once more.

The funny thing is that tourists who visited Yellowstone in the summer and choose to visit Jackson in the winter, perhaps for the downhill skiing, may be taking pictures of some of the same elk in both places. They might not recognize the elk from previous encounters, but they might well be the same animals on winter holiday.

The National Elk Refuge was established in 1912 as a sanctuary for elk next to Jackson Hole, spread over nearly twenty-five thousand acres. The land mass is large enough that it borders the town, the Bridger-Teton National Forest, and Grand Teton National Park. At times over the years, as many as twenty-five thousand elk wintered there, though in more recent years the number has diminished to about seven thousand five hundred per season.

The attraction, from the start, was easy access to food. The grassy plains area received less snow than many other spots in the region and thus the eats were easier to get at with less digging involved. As winter receded and snow melted, the elk gradually move on, roaming back to where they came from, ready to resume a fresh cycle of life.

However, there is not enough natural food for so many thousands of elk to survive and an important, integral feeding program was instituted as a supplement, with regular feeding times administered by humans. At times, by special lottery, some elk may be hunted, and the high cost of obtaining such a permit provides funding for the program.

A symbol of Jackson Hole's connection to the elk and the refuge is the town square. Each of the entrances to the George Washington Memorial Park at four street corners features an antler arch overhead that people stroll under. There are an estimated ten thousand to twelve thousand pounds of antlers contained in the arches. The arches themselves are surely more commonly photographed than the elk located a few miles away.

The elk range itself is just off a highway, fenced in, but the animals don't come up close

As do many of the animals in Yellowstone National Park, elk spend a great deal of their waking hours gorging on readily available vegetation.

to the fencing, instead wandering on the flat ground, snow-covered in winter, just far enough away so that they are not ready-made photo subjects. It's almost as if they are business partners, in cahoots with the visitor center.

For twenty-five dollars, tickets can be purchased at the Jackson Visitor Center for individuals to take horse-drawn sleigh rides onto the refuge grounds and mingle with the elk fairly up close for the type of pictures rarely captured of elk anywhere else. Used to the operation, the elk gather in bunches and lie about in peaceful rest as the sleighs pull closer than would otherwise be tolerated in the wild. They still need their space and if an invisible boundary is crossed, they will rise and depart, snubbing those who paid for the privilege of taking those pictures. For the most part, without disruption, the sleigh ride is a sixty-minute photo extravaganza of a guided tour.

The horses were two-thousand-pound pullers, one particular duo called Daniel and Boone. No one had to ask the origin of the names or why the two were partners. Occasionally, to seize the spotlight, a bull elk stood and bellowed a loud grunting sound. Mothers and young ones tended to laze around. They were watchful, but not skittish. Guides delivered nonstop informational talks as the horses pulled groups of perhaps fifteen people into this close-up situation.

Actually, elk began making this area a winter gathering area many years before the situation was formalized with the refuge. They became vacation regulars as far back as the 1880s. In the early 1900s it became apparent that although the elk kept coming, the food supply was dwindling. Rather than watch a mass starvation event unfold, a photographer-conservationist named Stephen Leek took up the cause. He not only snapped pictures to accompany his words but

This broad-shouldered, muscular guy definitely looks like the king of his domain.

traveled widely, giving lectures explaining the circumstances to public gatherings and rousing public support.

Wyoming's state legislature responded first, finding five thousand dollars in its budget to buy hay for the elk, and then in 1911 Congress entered the picture, donating twenty thousand dollars for food. A year later the refuge was established and it has been an elk stronghold since. Although it is not much discussed, since this is an elk zone, about one thousand bison are also known to spend time wintering in the same locale, sharing the twenty-five thousand acres. They mind their own business and no one kicks them out.

Jackson has adopted these elk and is protective of the herds. People know they must be fed at times since the grasses run out or become too snow-covered. The refuge brings people to Jackson for visits, which make the elk partners in tourism. The residents make money, the elk get food. They work together, though no contract was ever signed.

Since 1968, an annual auction of shed antlers has been conducted. The local Boy Scouts go around the refuge retrieving the antlers the bulls leave behind. Once collected, they are turned over to officials who conduct a fundraising auction. Some 75 percent of the money from the auctions goes towards habitat improvement for the elk. The other 25 percent goes to Friends of Scouting.

The sleigh rides for paying customers began in 1965. The guides are US Fish and Wildlife Service concessionaires, much like the business operators who sell food inside national parks. A spokeswoman for the service said about thirty thousand people a year take the sleigh rides. At twenty-five dollars a head, that comes out to $750,000, which can help defray some expenses.

"For some people, it's the closest they get to wildlife," said the service spokeswoman. "The

The lawn always seems comfortable at Mammoth Hot Springs despite the large amount of human traffic in the area.

elk are pretty acclimated to people. It's pretty unique."

As in American national parks themselves, visitors come from all over the world to see the elk in the refuge, to take their up-close photographs and see the animals in the wild. Some people so appreciate the experience they come back again the same day for another hour. Or they return a day later to take the tour all over again.

The elk don't seem to mind being so actively photographed. They probably have heard those camera clicks one hundred thousand times each. When winter ends, the snow melts, and the season changes, the elk also melt away into the surrounding forests where once again there are plenty of greens to eat. And many of the elk make their way to their real homes in Yellowstone.

The colors may differ, but Yellowstone on a sunny day in winter can still offer impressive scenic views.

CHAPTER 13
The Yellowstone Snowcoaches

The snow was thick outside the window as late afternoon darkness fell in Yellowstone National Park. The combination of the early nightfall on Christmas Eve and precipitation meant it was difficult to see far as the large yellow snowcoach rolled along at twenty miles per hour.

Sightseeing was finished for the day for lack of visibility. Bears were in hibernation anyway at this time of year. Wolves were their usual reclusive selves. Elk had been seen, but not in abundance. Bison, as always bosses of their domain, had drifted in and out of the picture all day. Now they were hunkering down, just being drifted in, their bodies collecting snow, their faces being turned into snowy masks as they furrowed beneath the top layer of snow for something to eat.

The park in winter is a very different animal than it is in summertime. Park roads are not plowed. Family vehicles are not invited in. Several entrances are closed for the season. But Yellowstone is still Yellowstone, offering a different side of itself, a winter wonderland at its best. Even in a storm, there was something spellbinding about the historic place. The forest was a silent wall. Mountains were half-obscured, half-visible as the wind whipped and the whiteness piled up.

There was still something magical about Yellowstone, even in the meanest of seasons, in the worst of weather. For the athletic and energetic, the park offers cross-country skiing and snowshoeing opportunities. Snowmobile tours can be arranged. For those who are older and less likely to dare the elements and prefer comfort over exercise, there are snowcoaches.

Yellowstone in winter is not for everybody. Many Americans, and many tourists from elsewhere, are not lured by snowed-in wintry places. They would rather stay in their living rooms and watch television, or sit by the fire with a brandy. For those of more adventurous spirit, a Yellowstone tour can be heady and pleasurable. Compared to the crowds of summer, attendance is much lower. Approximately 3 percent of annual visitors show up daily in winter versus on a given day in the summer.

However, it was recognized more than a half-century ago that there was a growing curiosity amongst Yellowstone aficionados as to what it was like to view the park in winter. Two decades into the twenty-first century, the snowcoaches

Traveling by snowcoach in Yellowstone is a decades-long tradition, a mode of transportation that gives winter visitors a fresh look at the park while staying warm.

could generally be described as fourteen-passenger yellow vans with rubber tracks instead of tires for mobility, causing some observers to compare them to tank treads. Park concessionaires had deals with the National Park Service to provide tours, one of them running from Mammoth Hot Springs to Old Faithful and back, a distance of one hundred miles during a day. Likewise, trips were offered from Jackson Hole, from the other direction.

An historically famous style of vehicle being phased out was called a Bombardier. The machines covered the roads on what seemed to be more like oversized skis. The sturdy vehicles were smaller than the coaches, and older. They had been reliable touring vehicles since 1952, but the celebrated last run took place in 2016 as they headed into retirement. One by one, the Bombardiers were sold off, fetching as much as ten thousand dollars. Certainly the appeal was there to the car collector fraternity and nostalgia lovers.

The modern world had passed the Bombardiers by. They cost too much to repair and keep in running order, and later generations of similar vehicles better served the touring public with larger windows, firmer tread, and more power. There was also the issue of environmental demands. The older vehicles did not meet emission standards, so they were polluting air quality in the park. Their passing did provoke nostalgia for an age gone by, though, especially from drivers who became attached to them despite a certain lack of power steering that meant much arm strength was needed to guide them.

"It is the end of an era in many ways," said Rick Hoeninghausen, who was director of

Bison must put up with often-terrible winter weather conditions as they try to survive until the next spring.

marketing for Xanterra, the large Yellowstone concessionaire.

The background issues aside, tourists gravitated toward the Bombardiers because of their old-school feel. But many who took snowcoach rides did not know the difference, or the history. It's pretty cozy inside the more recently manufactured snowcoaches, and especially inside the really modern new ones. It is warm enough inside the coaches for visitors not only to unzip their winter coats, but to take them off.

Gazing out the window, a half-dozen travelers were energized by the sight of three bison standing in the road. Their faces were half-obscured by fresh snow. Bison don't seem to be much bothered standing around in snowfall. Sometimes they can be seen foraging, noses deep into the snow cover, penetrating to the roots below. They raise their mighty heads chewing, causing laughter to the onlooker because it appears they are wearing Halloween disguises.

The amount of wildlife readily noticed from the windows of a coach in winter is much smaller than what is likely to be seen from the windows of a car in summer over the same span of time. However, on one ride two viewers took note of bison, coyote, ducks, and a bald eagle. This ticking off the checklist occasioned commentary. The coyote sighting excited several. Those people thought it was a wolf. The driver-guide didn't want to burst the bubble and kept quiet for a while. After a pause, she said, "Did you want it to be a wolf?" A passenger replied, "Of course." The guide said, "Okay, it's a wolf." But it wasn't. Shucks.

The weather can change swiftly in the park, and it did on a day that began under cloud cover and ended in a mini-blizzard. "Welcome to winter down here," the driver said. "Last week when I drove around, I was pretty much driving on grass. The cold is our friend."

It was twenty-five degrees Fahrenheit outside, not extreme cold, though just enough to encourage the snow. The snowcoach did not glide, nor did it provide as smooth a ride as car commercials say about a company's new model. It lurched.

The snow on the road was uneven, making for some holes and bumpy stretches that not even tracks could avoid.

By 2020, the thirty-three coaches being used for the tours were new and up-to-date with better tread, bigger windows, and more efficient engines. They resembled fancy school buses, though only holding slightly more than a dozen passengers, not an entire class.

Winter tours of Yellowstone originated with officials in surrounding communities asking the National Park Service to plow the roads. Starting in the 1930s, the towns began getting requests for winter tourism—a way for them to make money during down times—and they wanted the business. Whether they just wanted to give the park a rest for part of the year, did not want to provide more staffing in the winter, or some other reason, the National Park Service deflected those asks for years.

It was not until 1949 that the National Park Service yielded to community lobbying and began plowing some snow in winter. The first snowcoaches appeared, passenger vans resting on skis. They were powered by airplane propellers. The Bombardiers then began a sixty-year run as the chief form of snowcoach, each capable of holding ten passengers on tour at a time. Those coaches were affixed to snow tracks and skis. There was some concern the windows were not large enough for appropriate viewing, but for many years the visitors had to make do that way with whatever could be seen of the grand landscape. Plus, guides made frequent stops to allow the riders to stretch their legs and see geysers and mountains unobstructed.

Travel by snowcoach is still available each winter in Yellowstone National Park, though tourists have to be adaptable. Snowcoach trips can be taken at the North Entrance, Mammoth Hot Springs, from Jackson, the South Entrance, or from West Yellowstone, the West Entrance. The trips do not cover the same terrain throughout the large park, though they may overlap at Old Faithful.

It is humorous to note the clientele at Old

Whether it is snow or frost, the trees in Yellowstone must be hardy to make it through the winter months.

Faithful depending on the time of year. In summer, when the park has thousands of people a day visiting, many hundreds, or even one thousand people might show up at Old Faithful at the same time for one of its regular eruptions. They may be attired in short-sleeved shirts, baseball caps, shorts, or Hawaiian shirts. In winter, the crowd may be one-tenth as large for a given eruption and the viewers might be heavily bundled against the weather, decked out in thick parkas, even snowmobile suits and helmets, heavy gloves, and knit hats. There is definitely less competition for seating at Old Faithful during the heart of the winter.

During a snowcoach stopover at Old Faithful, a tourist from Dallas, Texas, chose to sit on the benches provided, but realized it was not as comfortable as it would be in summer. "My butt is frozen," she said. One hazard of the game.

She was on a journey from Jackson Hole, one that began with a passenger van pick-up at her hotel and culminated a full twelve hours later with her being dropped off at her hotel in the dark. In between, the vans ferried her and others to a central transfer zone inside Yellowstone, where they shifted to the snowcoaches. The snowcoaches, which were of the newer variety, with larger windows, are not designed to travel on bare roads. They stick to the snow. The National Park Service and the concessionaires refer to the snowcoach trips, as well as snowmobile journeys, as "oversnow" tours.

The Jackson tour was a bit pricier than that from the North Entrance. Turns out there are some white snowcoaches, too, certainly capable of blending into the landscape. They had better not run off the road or they might become indistinguishable from snow banks.

More miles were covered from the Jackson side, but also more food was provided. Only a short distance into the trip that began at 6:00 a.m., the vans stopped at a central location for a hot breakfast. A hot lunch was also included later. Patrons were surprised they were not simply handed a sandwich and an apple, but were able to ingest a high-quality meal.

Although the coaches are heated, the riders step out often to stand by the road and gaze at landscape features, wildlife, and get close-up photos with steam pouring from geysers, so there is ample opportunity to chill the body. A hot meal is of psychological, as well as genuine, value. Besides, this trip to Old Faithful and back was one hundred twenty-five miles. There were hours to be spent in the coach.

A particular batch of half-dozen tourists were coincidentally all from Texas. They were not traveling in the same group, but in late December just happened to book vacations close to Christmas for a winter sojourn in Yellowstone. Back home the temperature was about sixty degrees Fahrenheit. In Yellowstone it ranged between twenty and thirty degrees. Many other Americans were headed to Texas instead for their own mild-weather vacations and were no doubt packing lighter.

A couple in their thirties from even balmier Houston could not make their family members understand why they wanted to head into a land of snow and ice. Those relatives were much more mentally attuned to the Caribbean. "Our family thought we were crazy," the female half of the duo said.

They agreed the solitude and quietude offered by a winter trip was more appealing to them than trying the larger crowds of summer. Statistics indicated the average Yellowstone attendance between 2012 and 2017 each July was 922,000 people, but in January during the same period it was 28,000. "A little bit of privacy," the same woman said.

Many bodies of water being passed, including the robust Yellowstone Lake, were frozen over, illustrations of just how cold it gets and can stay within the park. The lake looks large enough to avoid freezing, but that is not so.

As usually occurs on any such trip, someone asked the driver-guide if everything was going to blow up and kill them during a volcanic eruption while they were passing through. The questioner was assured there would be ample warning before the super volcano's big eruption.

In 2017, Yellowstone and Grand Teton were excellent vantage points for viewing the North American solar eclipse, and both of the parks were jam-packed with people at that time. The eclipse occurred in summer. No doubt winter attendance records would have been set if the eclipse happened on a different schedule. One of the guides jokingly connected the eclipse with a potential volcanic blast, saying a slogan could be developed such as, "I came for the eclipse and stayed for the eruption."

Snug in the coach, riders spied two hardier cross-country skiers pushing themselves over the snow along the road, and someone shouted, "Wildlife!"

Plenty of snow to go around whatever the terrain in Yellowstone National Park.

Winter exploring in Yellowstone on snowmobiles has undergone numerous rule changes over the years to limit the amount of exhaust and noise in the park, but a policy was finally settled on in the 2000s that satisfied most.

CHAPTER 14
Snowmobiles in Yellowstone

Snowcoaches are steered by professional drivers and guides "oversnow," as is said in Yellowstone. Snowmobiles are guided by individuals, either following professionals or on private trips.

Unlike the snowcoaches, which were pretty much the favorites, snowmobiles were much more controversial. In their early days of operation, they spewed fumes and they made a racket. If people wanted traffic, to smell gasoline, and to have conversation drowned out by engines, they could stay home in big cities. Yellowstone National Park was supposed to be more about finding peace and communing with nature.

Yellowstone had gone from stagecoaches to railroads to the automobile, but it wasn't until 1963 that the snowmobile was introduced to its 2.2 million acres in winter. That first year just six snowmobiles entered the park. They were noticed, but not an issue.

However, as snowmobiles were improved and backcountry riding became more popular, Yellowstone became a major destination for riders. Driving a snowmobile did not require a smooth road. In fact, snow was necessary for a smooth ride. Theoretically, one could drive a snowmobile just about anywhere in the park, though not all areas were legal.

By the late 1990s, an average of 795 snowmobiles per winter day came into Yellowstone for recreational riding. A backlash developed. There was concern too many snowmobiles heavily contributed to air pollution in the park. That caused worry not only about the long-term air quality, but of effects on plant life and even wildlife.

Over time, tensions increased over what was perceived to be the proper number of snowmobiles to allow into the park and how many were too many. Winter tourism kept expanding and the visitor count over the cold season grew to more than one hundred thousand. At one point, some sixty thousand snowmobiles were counted entering the park, and by 1997 they had two hundred miles of groomed trails available to them.

Simultaneously, and again to the consternation of conservationists and the park's managers, the bison population began dropping. The animals began walking along the trails and following paths right out of the park. This put them in jeopardy. The bison did not actually say they were bothered by the noise and pollution, but the results were the same as they meandered away, sometimes to their deaths.

Animal rights and health-oriented organizations filed lawsuits asking for federal studies of winter recreation inside the park and the ripple effects that could harm certain species. Those who ran operations that provided snowmobile tours felt they were being discriminated against and were fearful they would be run out of business. There was some disagreement about just how valuable this business had become, but estimates ran into the millions of dollars. Tourists spent their dollars at hotels in the communities on the outskirts of the park, ate in local restaurants, bought souvenirs, and spent money on their guided snowmobile trips. Of course, others came to Yellowstone with their own snowmobiles, though they also spent dollars using the local facilities.

The flip side was represented by the conservationists who questioned whether too many snowmobiles flouted the fundamental Yellowstone mission of preserving the park for the enjoyment and pleasure of future generations if air pollution ruined things and signature animals like bison were harmed or had their long-term survival jeopardized.

Yellowstone is located at 6,600 feet of elevation—and higher—so the entire park receives a generous helping of snow from early fall into the spring.

Arguments and battles seesawed within administrative agencies and in the courts, dragging on for years. At one point the presidential administration of Bill Clinton intended to ban snowmobiles altogether from Yellowstone and neighboring Grand Teton National Park. The policy was not enacted and the matter was taken up by the administration of President George W. Bush.

Conservationists demanded all snowmobiles be prohibited. Outdoor recreational advocates wanted unlimited snowmobile access to Yellowstone for their rides.

Environmentalists were looking forward to a cap they thought might help the situation. However, when a cap was announced, the high number of snowmobiles permissible per day came off as shocking. A new rule took effect in December 2003, but it allowed up to 1,100 snowmobiles into Yellowstone daily. Neither side

gave up warring, and the tangling continued for what seemed to be an eternity.

From the first rumblings of serious discontent and challenges, it took fifteen years to work out the rules by which Yellowstone now operates. Seven different plans had been proposed over those years and they had all been challenged in court. This was very much a bitter battle for those who felt they were standing up for their individual freedoms to visit the park in the manner they wished, and those who believed they were doing the right thing in protecting the park.

Peace was brokered in 2013 when the federal government approved a plan taking effect in December 2014. As of that date, the number of snowmobile groups was capped at fifty-one per day, with no more than ten riders in a single group. The single most important development contributing to a new plan was the evolution of the snowmobile itself. The industry modified, reshaped, and redesigned the machines to be more fuel and emissions efficient, much as the automobile industry has changed over the decades. The newer models of snowmobiles had much less impact on air quality.

That was a huge breakthrough. Businesses that rented snowmobiles bought newer ones. Individuals who wished to drive in the park on their own got used to the rules supervising their private trips. The word spread they would not be allowed to cruise around the park unless they had up-to-date, modern machines. Spokesmen on both sides of the issue, the snowmobile industry on the perimeter of Yellowstone and those who viewed themselves as caretakers of the park, approved of the new program as an acceptable compromise.

The one commercially guided snowmobile company on the east side of the park is Gary Fales Outfitting, whose family has been guiding in the park by one method or another for decades. Fales and his family guided George H. W. Bush on a fishing trip shortly before he was elected president.

Fales operates a fleet of snowmobiles for the hardy winter visitor.

"It's a totally different experience in the winter," Fales said. "There's absolutely no crowds there. It's a winter wonderland and so special."

There is little doubt Yellowstone in winter is not the same as Yellowstone in summer. They are like two people, one cloaked in snow, one courting sunshine; fraternal twins, it might be said. Anyone who has experienced both seasons is quite clear on that. One guide, Jim Key, who was a Yellowstone regular for decades, first visited the park in 1962 and was married in the park in 1964.

"People ask me which is better, winter or summer," Key said. "They're just different. The park takes on a whole different personality in the winter."

It can be slow going walking through deep snow for animals like this coyote that are built low to the ground.

The last several years have been benign. Selected concessionaires won the right to guide private groups into the park and that method has proven quite popular. During the course of a day snowmobiles and snowcoaches periodically overlap, the individuals who chose to drive themselves and those who chose to leave the driving to others seeking their own levels of comfort.

Individuals also designed their own trips. As of December 2014, people who owned the necessary quality snowmobile could take their own trip, without a guide, stopping their machines where they chose to, as long as they had applied for and received permits.

In January 2015, a middle-aged couple from Cody, Wyoming, rented a modern snowmobile and took a two-day, 160-mile trip riding together, minus guides. They enjoyed the scenery, seeing the bison, and whatever other wildlife they could see. They were on their own—legally. They were local pioneers, pretty much the first non-guided riders from that part of the ecosystem under the new system. The Wyoming riders' journey came under an umbrella heading for the day, counting as one of a maximum of one hundred ten "transportation events."

That meant the private couple's ride was lumped together with commercially guided trips and their snowmobiles. There was also a small-print part of the contract that the snowmobilers committed to driving a machine that represented the best available technology. By definition, that meant they had to use a modern machine, not any old dilapidated one that had been parked in the garage in storage since the 1970s.

A National Park Service spokesman at the time the new program kicked into gear said officials had a lot of explaining to do for people applying for permits who hadn't quite assimilated that aspect of the system. "We've spent a great deal of time telling people they can't [just use their old models]."

The oversnow snowmobile speed limit is thirty-five miles per hour. The Cody couple was enthralled by the quiet and the absence of other snowmobiles and tourists nearby as they rode around the park, along the road, and all the way to Fishing Bridge. They were basically winter newcomers experiencing the park with fresh eyes. The man had not been in Yellowstone in winter in ten years, and the woman had been inside during the winter once as a youth, but remembered little about that excursion. They saw almost no one else for miles at a time, an impossibility in the summer. An exciting moment occurred when they saw a wolf pretty up close. "He jumped the guardrail right in front of us," the man said. Truly a rare experience.

Naturally enough, the largest number of people they saw at one place was Old Faithful, but not even at Fountain Paint Pot, often crowded in summer, was anyone around. They counted swans on the ride until they stopped at sixty. They saw as many as fifty bison in a herd. Coyotes and mule deer crossed their path.

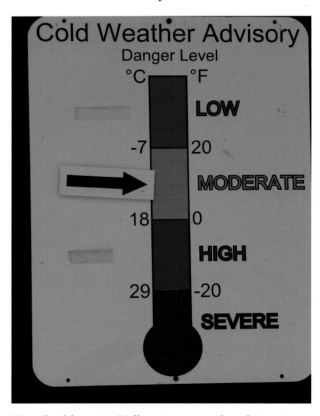

Most buildings in Yellowstone are closed in winter, but one can read the temperature on a small stopover place much smaller than the summer concession stations.

The temperature was minus seven degrees when the trip started and they noted a minus-twelve-degree temperature at one point. Snowmobile suits are snug and warm, though, and no complaints were made about winter's effects. At times the wind kicked up and swirled snow obscuring the route, and while being alone in the park was the entire point of the trip, the potential danger when something like that occurred was a reminder of the risks of riding without others. At some times, the man said, he was driving blind, or as he put it, steering "by Braille."

Yet they also felt they would be the envy of others who had not chosen a similarly risky vacation of solitude. "It felt like a dream we were even there," he said. "I thought, 'I wonder what are all the other people doing?'"

The other people, those they knew, were home, at work, or building an indoor fire. But there were snowcoaches and snowmobile groups in the park having approximately the same experiences as those Wyoming folks.

More groups set out as teams on snowmobiles, many of the drivers either first-time riders or quite inexperienced. They mostly took day trips, gathering before first light and returning to their staging bases after dark, but not too late for dinner. Whether individual drivers, or group tourists, everyone remained just as fascinated by bison as summer visitors. There were few of them out and about, but many found themselves displaying those snowy masks on their faces. Other bison hunkered down near steam vents close to geysers. The earth was warmer. It was the human version of reclining by the fireplace. Other times the bison would stroll down the middle of the road. As always, the animals had the right of way. Eight riders paused by the side of one road to gaze at a solitary bison that might well have weighed 1,200 pounds. It was not on the move, but if they had come any closer they might have provoked it.

On one peculiar day this band of snowmobilers had every kind of weather that seemed possible. The sun came out. The clouds came out. The sky shone blue. The sky turned gray. The air was clear. Then it snowed. The air was calm. Then the wind howled. Visibility offered beautiful vistas. Then the riders were in a whiteout, unable to see the road more than twenty yards ahead. Hands gripped the handlebars of the snowmobiles more tightly. The guide bunched up the riders to make sure nobody got separated from the pack.

One feature of the snowmobiles unknown to the novices was that the handlebars were heated. Even wearing gloves, fingers could freeze and grips could slip, so this was a useful option. Otherwise going even thirty-five miles per hour in a slight wind could provoke frostbite. The wind was not steady and briefly the sun was so bright one teenager stripped down to bare chest, freeing himself of the snowmobile-suit top, sweater, and shirt. That lasted only moments before parents and the guide intervened to eliminate such foolishness inherent in underestimating the elements. His simple comment was, "I was hot."

This was a day trip of about one hundred miles round-trip. The guide was Terry Dolan, who at that point in his career had led about five hundred Yellowstone snowmobile trips. Talk about someone who has seen everything. Dolan was even at the ready when the straggler in the group lost just enough control of the steering to glide off the side of the road and get stuck in a snowbank. In attempting to rev the engine and push out, the snowmobile overturned and pinned the driver's leg against the snow. He could not lift the machine off his leg. It took only seconds for Dolan to ride to the rescue. He might have been seven people away, but he noticed the mishap immediately.

The outfitter had proclaimed no experience was necessary in driving a snowmobile, which was at least partially true for most, but was not a sure-thing recommendation for everyone. It was possible to go for hours on end as a beginner, but maybe a little bit longer day than it should be for a first-timer. It was not that much of a strain, but the body, back, and arms could well be aching the next day.

One reason for Fales's and Dolan's comments

Winter, spring, summer, or fall, Old Faithful geyser still keeps to its eruption schedule for visitors.

about how easy it was to drive a snowmobile was the fact that it started with the push of a button. It was not necessary to rev the engine and step on the gas as one does with a car.

Six members of the group belonged to the same family from Illinois. They had never before been to Yellowstone in winter. While some were younger teens, the parents and the older siblings drove their own snowmobiles while the younger ones held on to drivers' waists. They didn't even have to push the start button.

Never mind Illinois, this particular guide had already hosted winter tourists from China, Australia, and Italy. Those with adventurous hearts come from everywhere.

This team did not cross paths with many people, only a few snowcoaches and one other snowmobile group at Canyon Village, which in the summer is its own bustling metropolis. That's all. The mom in the Illinois group said the self-contained nature of the tour and the lack of

crowds gave the circumstances a self-sufficient feel. "It feels like we're our own gang," she said.

These Yellowstone novices loved what they experienced. Their clothing was tough enough they never got cold, even when the air did and the wind blew. "The best way I can describe it," said the dad, "is it was like having a pass to Disneyland."

A wild Disneyland of the winter.

To some degree, that crew had it easy, with a guide for the snowmobile tour, appropriately heavy gear, and a one-day visit. But there are park people who have lived and worked year-round in Yellowstone. That means they take what they get from winter. That was true of so-called first ranger Harry Yount, the US Cavalry, and National Park Service officials.

When he was a youth, Richard Jones's family lived in the park in winter. His father Bob was a ranger and in the 1950s was assigned to clear snow off roofs of cabins and perform many solo tasks. In 1956, a magazine story about the family was published with the headline, "They Could Be the Loneliest Family in America." The magazine, called *Household*, did not survive. The family did.

Richard Jones, who grew up to become a park ranger himself, although not in Yellowstone, said he was about six years old at the time and remembers the snow seemingly almost always being over his head. "Of course, I wasn't very tall."

There are not many people spread around Yellowstone during the winter. Most of the roads are not plowed, so cars are not on tour the way they constantly are on Grand Loop Road during peak months from June to September. The snowmobiles travel in packs, so they might be there one minute and gone the next in terms of traffic. Silence may descend quickly once the machines disappear over the hill.

Sunshine may offer the illusion of warmth, but that reality is that some of the coldest days inside the park may occur when the sky is bright blue. The air can be stunningly crisp and venturing out to admire the winter beauty can risk frostbite without hats, gloves, and thick parka coats for protection. One awaiting Old Faithful's eruption in winter may be dressed in immobilizing gear, but standing or sitting still may feel frozen.

Even outdoorsmen have a peculiar relationship with winter. For all of those who love to fish on open water, some 90 percent of them would rather recline at home in the living room than take themselves ice fishing. That is the mentality of most Americans. There is weather you can enjoy outdoors and weather you avoid by staying indoors.

Of course, there is a robust alpine skiing industry, and skiers of a different sort, the cross-country skiers with a kinship to Scandinavian countries, do enjoy the backcountry, especially in

There is so much snow in Yellowstone (varying by areas within the park), sometimes hundreds of inches at a high elevation, that the National Park Service keeps an eye on avalanche-susceptible areas.

Alaska, Montana, Wyoming, New England, or the Upper Midwest. They are people not easily intimidated by winter.

It took decades for Yellowstone officials to respond to what was at first a limited demand from the public for winter tourism, but despite all the brouhaha over snowmobile use, snowcoaches always provided the most appeal. Snowcoaches were a brilliant idea and compromise.

Rather than drive a snowmobile bundled up against the adventure, more tourists were intrigued to see the winter wild of Yellowstone at a different level of comfort. They were willing to bundle up, but not be exposed directly to the elements, wind, snow, and cold at its whim. A snowcoach was the obvious and perfect compromise. A guide who knew how to drive the big machines was provided, and the guide provided information to the visitor from Alabama or Arizona who had practically never seen snow except in photographs. The riders were still mobile, but indoors. There was a heater that spewed forth warmth, somewhat like riding on a Greyhound bus.

And those picture windows, bigger than ever as the 2000s turned to the 2020s, offered tremendous views of bison along the side of the road, an elk crossing the street, or the occasional wolf stealthily sneaking around in the timber. You could see it all without risking frostbite.

Not every park entrance has a concessionaire operating the snowcoaches, but one could pick up a ride at Mammoth Hot Springs, on the Gardiner, Montana side, or in Jackson Hole, on the Wyoming side, or in West Yellowstone. The trips were organized so no one missed out on a stop at Old Faithful. The geyser was always a not-to-be-missed attraction, especially for the first-time visitor.

It was a much longer ride from Jackson than from Mammoth, operators piling tourists into vans in the early morning, cutting through Grand Teton and exploring on the opposite end of the park, but that meant there was merely more time to break for snacks along the way.

The curiosity factor is a driver of attention bringing people to Yellowstone in any season, but especially winter. What is remote Yellowstone, its woods and wildlife, like when the air is frigid and the snow is deep? Some people must find out in person. They have usually, though not always, first been to Yellowstone in summer when the air is warmer, there are more people, and the wildlife is more easily seen.

Yet winter has its charm: the quiet, the peace, the beauty of a landscape coated in snow. Many of the trees are evergreen and it has been commented that whole areas resemble Christmas-tree farms.

Bison still populate the park in winter. They have a tougher time scrounging for food, insinuating their noses and mouths through top layers of snow to reach grass and plants beneath. They must work harder for their meals, for sure. Some also hang out near thermal features, gathering some of the heat thrown off by the steam, sometimes sprawling on ground warmed by the activity from below or next door. They are imitating Truman Everts by instinct. One might wonder just how long the bison remain in one spot soaking up the thermal feature by-product.

Winter is part of the cycle of the natural world and it takes its toll on the old and the weak, trimming the wildlife populations. Those animals which cannot fend for themselves by finding food, staying warm, staying healthy until the thaw comes may perish from the harshness of the climate.

For them, winter is not nearly the lark that summer living is inside Yellowstone when the sun is stronger, the food more abundant, and the lifestyle easier.

When it snows in Yellowstone, it makes it just that much harder for animals to forage for food.

This Yellowstone sign marks the boundary at each entrance to the park.

CHAPTER 15
Seasonal Openings

The sheer volume of snowfall, which differs at different elevations and in different areas of Yellowstone National Park, determines long-term, spring-summer seasonal accessibility within the 2.2 million acres.

Only a small portion of the park is open for exploration through those "oversnow" modes: snowcoach, snowmobile, and even cross-country skiing and snowshoeing. There are segments of territory within the park's borders that receive six hundred inches of snow annually, making those areas inaccessible for long periods of time.

The length of winter and the volume of snow also regulates the opening of the summer season. If it keeps right on snowing past the dates the National Park Service has set for opening day through a certain entrance, then that entrance will remain closed because the road is impassable, though there is at least some urgency to clear things up.

Yellowstone has five entrances monitored by the National Park Service, where admission is charged during the day, though anyone can ride into the park after daily staffing ceases. There is the North Entrance, through Gardiner, Montana; the Northeast Entrance, through Cooke City and Silver Gate, Montana; the West Entrance, through West Yellowstone, Montana; the East Entrance, through Cody, Wyoming; and the South Entrance, through Jackson Hole, Wyoming and Grand Teton National Park.

Gardiner is an exceptionally busy entrance, where the Roosevelt Arch is located, and which leads visitors to Mammoth Hot Springs. Cooke City and Silver Gate are tiny towns that are completely snowed in during the winter, though at other times are sometimes an alternative to the eastern approach. But that Northeast gate

entryway leads to the Lamar Valley, which teems with wildlife, especially bison; antelope are most readily seen in this area of the park.

Almost the entire fifty-mile drive from Cody on the east side is very much like already being inside the park. The terrain is identical, and often enough various animals wander into this area, particularly grizzly bears, some bison, the occasional moose, and sheep. Only a few miles outside the gate is Pahaska Tepee, the historical group of buildings where Buffalo Bill Cody brought hunters during the early days of the park's operation.

Buffalo Bill shrewdly surmised the immediate accessibility to Yellowstone from the east would benefit the city of Cody, and even now, more than a century after his death, his old cabin, next door to a restaurant and gas station, is visited by tourists in the still-rural country.

The community of West Yellowstone abuts the park on the west side, in Montana, and the connecting road bleeds right into the entrance gate with a simple turn. The busy South Entrance takes the visitor from Jackson Hole through Grand Teton on the John D. Rockefeller Jr. Memorial Parkway. That road is named for that member of the famous Rockefeller family because of the generosity of his donations to the National Park System.

It makes for a very long day to attempt to tour the entire park by automobile all at once. Yellowstone is best swallowed in day-long gulps focused on different regions. Much of the park opens for the summer before the end of April, although the East Entrance does not open until the first week in May. Not all roads open at once, however. Interference from left-over or late-falling snow can affect opening dates from the east side especially, because while the road does lead swiftly to Yellowstone Lake and Fishing Bridge, it climbs to 8,524 feet at Sylvan Pass.

It can snow at Sylvan Pass on just about any day of the year, but spring snow is common. Dangerous avalanche conditions can be created, and the National Park Service closely monitors the situation at the pass. Sometimes rangers fire off artillery cannons to bring down loosening snow resting on steep mountain sides so they do not give way on their own schedule and wreck passing cars.

Even after the park highway is plowed down to the asphalt surface, the handiwork of the workers can leave gigantic snow berms lining the road on both sides, some easily piled twelve feet high, well above the heads of individuals, cars, and even vans or buses.

Dunraven Pass at 8,859 feet of elevation is another area of Yellowstone where spring snow-melt comes only gradually and where early-season

plowing leaves monstrous berms alongside the road. Dunraven is the highest road pass within the park and is very susceptible to frequent snow-fall, at least as much so as Sylvan Pass.

The famous in-park lodges for the most part are not even open for business at this time.

One by-product of the iffy nature of the spring weather and the scheduled opening days through different entrances to the park is how those early-season openings have become special occasions for locals and those who live nearby in Wyoming and Montana. School is still in session throughout most of the nation in April and May, so families that plan vacations are out of the picture at that time of the year. And if a complex and expensive plan is in place and the weather interferes, the trip can be spoiled. Not so for those who live within reasonable driving distance and who do not wish to stay overnight.

To a certain degree, the Yellowstone season

Waiting to enter Yellowstone on opening day from the East Entrance, cars line up for as much as a half mile in early May.

opening has become a holiday of sorts for the park's neighbors. Also, many of the park personnel stationed at gates are longtime employees and recognize the annual regulars, making for a mini-reunion of sorts.

Dennis Lenzendorf had become the symbol of the East Entrance to many visitors. He was a presence year after year as his thirty years of National Park Service wound down to retirement. He lived on the premises, in a National Park Service house less than a hundred yards from the entrance, which had a gate across the front like a railroad track gate.

People often begin lining up at the East Entrance in small numbers in the middle of the night prior to opening day, some of them on purpose with hopes of being the first admitted through this gate for this season. When the time reached 8 a.m., Lenzendorf opened the barrier gate and said aloud, "Another year begins." It wasn't as if there were mobs of media on hand,

though there were a few journalists present to record the moment. And it wasn't as if the crowds were massing at the gate, though some years there were a substantial number of vehicles. People waited patiently for admittance in their cars as their turn to drive in approached.

The rangers made the same announcement as each vehicle rolled up: "Welcome to Yellowstone."

One fifty-six-year-old man from Billings, Montana, which was closer to the Cody-side entrance than some Montana entrances, said, "This is where I want to be" on opening day. He said he had been a Yellowstone visitor since he first came with family members and always chose to enter the park through this entrance. "All my life," he said. "I started when I was a kid."

He believed (and he was hardly alone with this thought) that Yellowstone was paradise. He loved the place and all it offered. "If there is a better place on earth," he said, "I haven't found one yet."

Spectacular foliage colors spread throughout the park in autumn.

Not everyone showed up exceptionally early. Many of the first visitors drove up knowing what time the gate opened and they were prepared to wait in line for a while. Both they and Lenzendorf, who was in his ninth season as chief gatekeeper, were a little bit surprised in 2016. The line stretched for a long way, as if the spirit of the one hundredth anniversary celebration of the National Park Service was already in full swing.

That spring Yellowstone was coming off a record attendance year in 2015, and the number of visitors in Yellowstone and across the National Park System was growing. Lenzendorf predicted how busy the season would be based on an opening-day analysis. It was not much different than making sports team predictions as the Major League Baseball or National Football League teams were in training camps.

It was not much of a risk going into 2016 to anticipate bigger crowds because of the anniversary of the establishment of the National Park Service, since considerable effort had gone into promoting the occasion. Right away that first morning Lenzendorf saw license plates representing South Dakota, Nebraska, Texas, Colorado, Missouri, and Florida, in addition to Montana and Wyoming. They could well have been senior citizens who wanted to come to Yellowstone ahead of the school's-out summer schedule.

"You can tell what kind of year it will be by opening day," Lenzendorf said. His prognosis was right, too. Yellowstone set another attendance record in 2016. It also has been doing so with some regularity since.

At the ranger gate, visitors were handed maps of the park, a newsletter that noted where road construction was underway, producing likely delays, and warning papers reminding people to stay clear of wildlife that might gore them, run them down, or bite them. People wanting photographs still had to be reminded to be cautious about getting too close before they snapped, or they could end up a casualty. "Look, but don't touch" is advice applied to animals, as well as landscape features.

Different features—the mountains, the rivers, Yellowstone Lake, the hiking trails, the geysers, the waterfalls—provide specific appeal to different people. They might appreciate it all, but something touches them about one natural aspect of the park. Showing up on opening day from the east side, "It's a tradition," one Cody woman said. She rose at 5:00 a.m. to get to the park early and armed with bear spray to take her annual solo hike.

One man in his sixties traveling with his wife said he first came to Yellowstone as a toddler, about four years old, with his parents. Then he took a half century off from the park. He didn't remember his youthful trip, but he had a checklist for this one, wanting to make sure he got a good eyeful of bison.

One element that drew a wolf out of hiding was an elk carcass. The wolf wanted food more than he wanted to remain out of sight and periodically emerged from trees to chomp at it. Whenever the animal appeared, visitors pulled off the road, creating a traffic jam. So many people wanted a glimpse a ranger had to be stationed on the scene to prevent spectators from getting too close and to stop them from snarling traffic in too major a way.

One set of parents from Fort Collins, Colorado, felt a national parks experience contributed to a well-rounded education, and they took their elementary-school-age kids out of class for an early-season Yellowstone trip.

There was no shortage of bison—thousands, spread across the landscape. It was also calving time, and the reddish-colored babies were learning to walk and run as they stayed close to their mothers.

One Cody resident named Daniel Bradford definitely sought to beat the rush each opening day on the east side. His goal was to arrive early enough to be the driver of the first car in line, although there was no prize for the distinction, and he had accomplished that a few times. He appreciated the quiet and the emptiness with the trees and surrounding hills.

"I like to walk around by myself," Bradford said. A half hour ahead of others was fine with

A golden glow suffuses the landscape in Yellowstone when the sun hits various mountain peaks.

him. By then he got itchy enough to pull out his camera and search for wildlife.

Another customer entering the park for a first time during a season kept a boat moored at Yellowstone Lake for the summer and regularly slept on it. He always had a bed, meaning there was no need to compete for hotel rooms or camping spaces.

One year, the journey by Cody-side visitors on opening day was sidetracked by a major attraction as they approached the East Entrance in the early morning. A grizzly bear was visible by the side of the highway. All it took was for one motorist to see it, leap out of the car bearing his camera, and a crowd formed.

The temperature was chilly about five miles from the park entrance, but the bear didn't mind. Everyone passing by screeched to a halt because, after all, as soon as they were allowed into the park they were going to look for wildlife like this. The bear didn't care where the park boundary was

and slipped out into similar terrain nearby. And he wouldn't have to pay the entrance fee when he wanted to go back into the park.

The bear appeared to have just awakened and it was remarked upon that it seemed to be stretching just like a human. "Yoga the Bear," teased Brian Perry, who was Lenzendorf's successor as the new chief ranger at the East Entrance.

Perry said the 2018 season seemed promising in terms of early bear activity. "It's a great time of the year to be in Yellowstone," he said. "We've been seeing lots of grizzly bears." Those are words visitors love to hear. Even veterans, such as the three women together at the front of car line, never tired of seeing grizzlies, though they said they once spotted nineteen of them in a single season.

Third in line behind this trio was Bradford, who may well have been number one again if he hadn't stopped to click off pictures of the out-of-park grizzly.

Even though the East Entrance opens the first week in May, there is still a snow warning posted. Sylvan Pass, at more than 8,200 feet, is only several miles down the road and could still receive fresh snow in May.

They don't give out awards for being first in line and there is no specific fame attached to it either, but people just make a little bit of fun out of the cachet of being the first. A woman with her young daughter was first in 2019, arriving at their spot by 3:00 a.m.

"I can't compete with that," Bradford said in another of his early bird years, though not as number one in line. Just like the year he stopped to photograph the bear, he stopped on the way to the gate this time because he saw a moose along the road. Moose are not terribly plentiful, so it was logical to take a picture when it could be taken.

One guy with his wife, from Lovell, Wyoming, turned the first-day Yellowstone visit into a tradition. He got into the habit of calling it an end to winter and start of a fresh season. "Mainly to see what's new out there," he said. Yellowstone was not going to change in a major way over the previous few months, but different wildlife might present themselves in May than had in October.

However, everyone who came early, who planned their day around the 8:00 a.m. gate opening, or was just anxious to enter the park, was thrown a curve. An unexpected snowfall hit Sylvan Pass and Perry was told to delay the gate opening as personnel plowed the road.

"It was forecast for sunny skies," Perry said. "We really weren't expecting the snow we got last night."

Sylvan Pass is only about seven miles beyond the east gate and there is no way for vehicles to get to the heart of the park from that direction without going over it. Perry had to inform motorists they were going to have to wait a little bit longer before they could enter Yellowstone that season.

The length of the delay turned into eighty minutes, though by the time the caravan of cars was allowed in and reached the pass, the sun was also helping melt the fresh snow and erase whatever road covering the plows had overlooked.

Fabulous sunsets in Yellowstone are icing on the cake of the scenery.

CHAPTER 16
For the Love of Yellowstone

Yellowstone National Park has stirred human emotions for hundreds of years. Those who stumbled upon it by accident at first, those who explored it by design, those who were enraptured by it after visiting on purpose and because they wished to see with their own eyes what others reported—all have begun love affairs with the park.

They are struck by the wonder of uniqueness. They are wooed by the splendor of vastness. They are thrilled by the scale of 2.2 million acres, or 3,500 square miles. They are impressed by the waterfalls, the rivers, the big lake, and the other lakes. They are astounded by the wildlife, the land's scope, its abundance, and simply its wildness.

Even if they have visited Yellowstone a hundred times, they keep coming back because of its specialness; because there is nothing like it near home, or most anywhere else; because they want others in their families to see what they have seen. They discover favorite activities: hiking, fishing, seeing marvels they can't duplicate either easily or at all in other locations. Just knowing they are in the world's oldest national park resonates in their minds.

Yellowstone moves people. It represents a piece of the American psyche, explains a story of the land, reveals an ancient and recent past, presents an endearing present, and promises a purity of a future that makes people feel good.

One of those people who spoke and wrote eloquently about ways that Yellowstone made him feel good was the naturalist John Muir, who probably spoke the earliest and spoke the loudest. "It is a big, wholesome wilderness on the broad summit of the Rocky Mountains," Muir wrote.

He referred to the attributes of Yellowstone as a park as being "full of exciting wonders. The wildest geysers in the world, in bright, triumphant bands, are dancing and singing in it, amid thousands of boiling springs, beautiful and awful, their basins arrayed in gorgeous colors like gigantic flowers. . . . Fortunately, almost as soon as it was discovered, it was dedicated and set apart for the benefit of the people."

People have been moved to write poetry about Yellowstone, including Lynne Bama, author of

There are many views available of the waterfalls at the Grand Canyon of the Yellowstone.

Yellowstone Rising. Her poems have such titles as "The Birth of Yellowstone," "View of Yellowstone Lake," "Mammoth Hot Springs," and "Grand Canyon of the Yellowstone."

In many poems she adopts the persona of Yellowstone figures such as explorer Joe Meek, Native Americans, and even a soldier's journal from the Washburn Expedition. Movingly, in one collection of verse, Bama became Truman Everts, the man who was lost and then rescued, writing in part:

> Somehow I knew I would be saved, if
> I could only struggle on despite the storm.
> The chill had pierced my very bones,
> and death was imminent
> when I saw two rough, but kindly
> faces looking down at me.
> *Are you Mr. Everts?*
> Yes, I answered,
> *all that is left of him.*

She had fun with the wonders of Mammoth Hot Springs, writing in part,

> What is this grace, this illusion
> of marble staircases, intricate galleries
> and burnished facades shaped by mere water
> bubbling out of cracks in a hill?

In such ways, Yellowstone brings out joy in visitors.

While it is well known that the photographs by William Henry Jackson helped turn the tide of congressional opinion in favor of making Yellowstone into a national park in 1872, it is little remembered at large that some of his photographs were destroyed in a fire.

However, although they were not printed in a publication, it seems more of them survived than was previously thought. In 2016, some one hundred forty years later, they came into the hands of the Buffalo Bill Center of the West in Cody, Wyoming.

Autumn brightens the trees in Yellowstone as leaves change colors.

The museum turned the pictures into a special exhibition, and many years after first intended, members of the public were able to enjoy them.

Whether hikers or anglers, repeat visitors to Yellowstone revel in the park in different ways. The something special that attracts one is not the same as what brings another. Also, Yellowstone at one time in their life may be frozen in their mind in a manner different than the experience they enjoy today.

One elderly man in his eighties from Powell, Wyoming, visited Yellowstone in the 1930s, and his family shot home movies of their trip. As older members of the clan died off, he inherited them. The films, somewhat sketchy in places but well-preserved in others, contained much footage of the bears in the park at a time when they were still being fed by humans, at the Lunch Counter and from cars. This man replayed the film for visitors and family alike, reliving the past from when he first saw the park. Even though he had visited countless other times and frequently took his own photographs, the old film touched something in him from his youth when all of those relatives depicted were still around.

Many times Yellowstone is visited by second- or third-generation families. The story is often told about how children brought to the park in the old family station wagon return towing their own kids in an SUV to introduce them to the same sights and sounds and wildlife. They hope the experience sticks with their own progeny and turns them into national park lovers.

On any given day in summer, newcomers flock to the park: those who have had Yellowstone on a family bucket list for years, those who wish to begin a tradition, or those who are following one. Three generations of one Wisconsin family—married couple, kids, and a mother-in-law—made the trek west. Number one on their hit parade was to see a bear. Almost immediately upon entering Yellowstone, their car found one. "Within five minutes," the father said.

This provoked a mild argument between dad and nine-year-old son, however. The kid was sure it was a grizzly; the man knew it was a black bear.

Crowds gather in great numbers in summer in anticipation of Old Faithful Geyser's eruptions.

"It was a black bear because that's what it was," he said, trying to cut off the debate.

Waiting for an eruption at Old Faithful was a honeymooning couple from Minnesota. "I came to see this," the woman said. It was hardly the worst honeymoon locale one could imagine.

The opening day of the fishing season may bring out a different crowd. A college student in his early twenties from Carlisle, Pennsylvania, carefully planned his job applications to have a summer job in Yellowstone for a couple of years in a row primarily to indulge his fly fishing passion. He was willing to work as a concessionaire for regular access to the bounty of the streams within the park, and he juggled his regular work schedule so he could be off to fish on the first day of the season.

One thing this fellow, Dillon Bennett, did not have to worry over was any long-distance driving to the fishing holes. He made his long drive to and from the park at the beginning and end of the tourist season but only had to drive minutes, or an hour tops, from where he was staying, within the park, to find world-class fishing.

He was out early and caught six cutthroat trout before the morning was gone on opening day of the 2019 fishing season. May 2019 set a record of 6.22 inches of rain in the week preceding the opener, and some snow flurries were mixed in. That just meant Bennett had to dress warmly.

Although the Yellowstone River was mere feet away, he preferred the tributary creeks for throwing his fly. Wearing waders, he advanced slowly through swirling waters. He was an earnest fisherman willing to put in time, explore slightly out-of-the-way places, and catch and release the beautiful fish at the heart of the Yellowstone fishery.

As an illustration of Yellowstone's wide appeal, a family from Mexico City was viewing Old Faithful one day. They had studied what Yellowstone offered well in advance of their trip and they had a checklist they carried around as they passed thermal features, waterfalls, and the wildest of wildlife. "We like to see what Mother Nature is capable of," the father said. Thus far they approved.

Motivations for journeying around Yellowstone, whether traveling thousands of miles to enter, or just a few to a specific destination spot like fisherman Bennett, were diverse. Some reasons included activities like fishing or hiking or boating. There was a desire to camp, celebrate a birthday or other holiday, or at long last to see what had been heard of for their whole lives from Yellowstone Lake to the Grand Prismatic Spring to Old Faithful. When the National Park Service conducted a survey, it found 87 percent of the visitors were from the United States. Americans were still in love with Yellowstone.

One seventy-two-year-old man had never been west of Pennsylvania before and was astonished by the landscape, the mountains, the waters, and the wildlife that did not run away from people the instant animals were spotted. "It's been an adventure," he said.

A twelve-year-old boy was visiting Yellowstone with his grandparents, and they saw a bear along the highway on the outskirts of the park. "Wow, a kid from Texas like me seeing a grizzly bear," the youngster said.

Two Americans, sixty years apart in age, who didn't even meet, though they overlapped at the grizzly, were blown away by the wildlife on the same day. Yet such a spontaneous gathering, organized by a bear, may well happen every day.

Jerry Mernin loved being a National Park Service ranger in general and a Yellowstone ranger in particular; he shared some of his hair-raising adventures in his book, *Yellowstone Ranger*. There was the time he and his wife, then living in the back of a ranger station, were awakened by a loud noise about midnight one night. It was a bear and cub on the front porch rummaging around and trying to break into their house.

Armed with a .44 Magnum handgun and a flashlight, he lost track of the grizzlies for a brief time, then had the adult bear hurl itself against the wall of the cabin trying to break in through a kitchen window. He was amazed when the window held. After about ninety minutes of keeping track, Mernin watched the bears settle down at the far end of the parking lot.

As soon as Mernin went back to bed, though, the big bear returned to the porch. By then

Birds perch on the Liberty Cap Cone at Mammoth Hot Springs.

Mernin had loaded a tranquilizer into a rifle and prepared for a different tactic if the bear did not simmer down. It did. The next morning, though, the bear was tranquilized and removed from the scene.

As a ranger in Yellowstone during the 1960s and 1970s, Mernin still spent some time on horseback patrolling. One of his most memorable assignments, he said, was accompanying President Jimmy Carter on his fishing trip to Yellowstone Lake in 1978. Even presidents get the itch to see Yellowstone up close, and throughout the history of the park several have stopped in.

Theodore Roosevelt visited more than once, and he dedicated the Roosevelt Arch at the Gardiner entrance in 1903 while laying a cornerstone for a Yellowstone road after a sixteen-day camping trip. He made a speech at the time:

Nowhere else in any civilized country is there to be found such a tract of veritable wonderland made accessible to all visitors, where at the same time not only the scenery of the wilderness, but the wild creatures of the park are scrupulously preserved, as they were, the only change being that these same wild creatures have been so carefully protected as to show a literally astounding tameness.

The creation and preservation of such a great natural playground in the interest of our people as a whole is a credit to the nation; but above all a credit to Montana, Wyoming, and Idaho.

President Chester Arthur rode a horse in Yellowstone. Gerald Ford visited Old Faithful prior to the 1976 election. Bill Clinton, Howard Taft, Calvin Coolidge, Franklin D. Roosevelt, and Warren Harding were among other presidents to absorb the magic of Yellowstone firsthand.

Carter did an Arthur. He rode a horse, and it belonged to Mernin. Mernin noted the logistical planning for Carter's entire visit was quite complex. Amy Carter, the president's daughter, was the first to catch a fish, a twenty-inch cutthroat trout, as the party circled the lake in separate canoes. Rosalynn Carter, the first lady, caught a few fish in her canoe, but Amy had the hot hand, catching several fish, one after the other. Finally, the president reeled one in. "A sigh of relief swept through the onlookers," Mernin wrote, "and everyone seemed to relax."

At the time, the superintendent of Yellowstone was John Townsley, whose father had also worked for the National Park Service. Mrs. Carter said the president was an accomplished horseman, and Townsley asked Mernin if Carter could ride his horse Eb. Townsley said his family had a photograph of his dad on horseback with Theodore Roosevelt, and he very much would like one of himself on horseback with this president. Carter got his ride and Townsley got his picture.

While rangers on horseback have become a thing of the past in Yellowstone, Bob Richard, a lifelong resident of nearby Cody, whose family has operated tours within the park over the years, and who has, along with relatives, shot thousands of photographs there, served as a Yellowstone ranger riding the range.

As part of his ranger duties in the 1950s, Richard rode horseback. The park was very good to Richard. Not only was he matched with a beloved horse named Big Red, he also met his wife in Yellowstone.

Yellowstone chief fisheries biologist Todd Koel examines statistics showing how many invasive lake trout have been removed from Yellowstone Lake over a recent period of time.

CHAPTER 17
Fighting for Fish

The prize fish is the cutthroat trout. The cutthroat has homecourt advantage in Yellowstone National Park. It has been present from the beginning and is such a symbol of the park that the National Park Service and its supporters go to extraordinary lengths to make certain the cutthroat sticks around.

When anglers come from afar to fish Yellowstone and its waters, most often they desire visits with the cutthroat. They can find other types of trout elsewhere, but the cutthroat is the lure, the fish that has first dibs on the mind and the terrain.

They are beauties as a fish, a member of the trout family that includes rainbow trout. The scientific name of the fish is *Oncorhynchus clarkii*, and the clarkii species name stems from William Clark of the Lewis and Clark Expedition.

Biologists and National Park Service officials take great pride in being the steward of the cutthroat within Yellowstone. But in the 1960s the cutthroat population was determined to be declining because of overfishing and the harvesting of too many eggs for hatchery use. A catch-and-release angling policy was implemented.

Then imagine the disappointment in 1994 when it was discovered the fish was facing a dire threat to its existence in Yellowstone Lake. Somehow, invasive lake trout had inappropriately been introduced to the body of water and were steadily destroying the population of cutthroat. It was almost surely the result of illegal introduction by a malevolent or careless individual or group of people. Bigger and stronger, the lake trout proliferated.

This latest blow to the cutthroat within the lake was by far the most damaging and portended extinction for the traditional species within that body of water. By 2000, the number of cutthroat in the lake had dropped to an alarming 10 percent of the level it had been in the early part of the twentieth century.

Attention turned to a monumental effort to rescue the revered cutthroat, turn the tide back in favor of that fish, and focus on a battle to perform the near-impossible by returning the lake's status to becoming more hospitable to cutthroat than to lake trout. Man was trying to undo what man had wrought by intervening in nature a second time.

Such efforts are costly, demanding, time-consuming, and present no guarantees about the future, but the National Park Service decided to draw a line and committed as many resources as possible to the fight against the lake trout, and also enlisted many sources of assistance.

Lake trout, per se, are not an unpopular fish. They are indeed a coveted fishing species elsewhere, sought by anglers in bodies of water where they belong, not where they are viewed as the enemy. Described as freshwater char in lakes in the northern Midwest, lake trout are a game fish in those areas and make for hefty and enjoyable meals. It is basically in Yellowstone Lake where lake trout have become dirty words, the bad guys of the water, because they thrive on eating cutthroat and decimating their freshly laid eggs after spawning.

While cutthroat may be six to forty inches in length, and a big one might tilt the scales to five pounds, the world-record lake trout caught on rod and reel was seventy-two pounds and measured just under five feet in length. Many exceed fifty pounds. It is not a fair fight between the two types of fish. Hence the despair and depression when lake trout were discovered as a new top-of-the-food-chain species in Yellowstone Lake.

Weapons have been aimed at lake trout eradication since 1994, at first with limited expenditures, and then with more time-intensive and financial commitments. Between that year and the late 2010s, it was estimated more than 2.3 million lake trout were removed from Yellowstone Lake. The total kept growing into the 2020s, with more efficient programs in place, with the removal skyrocketing to more than three million lake trout eliminated.

Scientists, government biologists, National Park Service fisheries experts, and volunteers turned lake trout elimination into a holy war, a war on several fronts employing many methods to alter the overall picture. Numerous ideas were considered and applied, or rejected, experimented with, or stuck with, over a period of many years in terms of providing the most effective assault on the invasive fish.

Officials were always open to new suggestions, willing to try out ways that could provide the biggest payoff of fish murder for the buck. Among other things, fisheries experts mounted an educational campaign to explain to the public why a species of fish that might otherwise be liked should be hated and run out of existence in this one lake.

"Lake trout are wonderful fish," a Yellowstone National Park biologist named Phil Doepke told one audience. "But they're not native to Yellowstone Lake."

By the second decade of the twenty-first century, studies had informed biologists that one adult lake trout would eat about forty-two cutthroat trout a year. That definitely showed what the cutthroat and their human allies were up against.

The creativity of the people fighting for the cutthroat was impressive as new ideas were tried. Schools of lake trout were victims of electroshocking to kill them. Gillnetting on a broad scale was implemented. Smothering lake trout spawning beds was another give-it-a-try program viewed as having some impact. Anything that could help

the cause was embraced, or at the least given an airing.

Angling policies favored the cutthroat. Yellowstone visitors could still fish on Yellowstone Lake, but it was catch-and-release for cutthroat while at the same time fishermen were required to keep or kill the lake trout caught. If they wished to take their lake trout catch home to eat, it was fine with the authorities. However, anglers could not simply throw the caught fish back in the water to swim again. It had to be killed first. This was a catch-and-kill program. Even if it was one fish at a time rather than a hundred caught in a gargantuan net at a time, this approach came under the every-bit-helps philosophy. It has been estimated between ten thousand and twenty thousand lake trout are caught by anglers annually, which is a fraction of the annual total of 350,000 to 400,000 removed, but still a fairly decent number of fish that would not otherwise be removed from the water.

Besides the insulting illegality of lake trout running off a signature Yellowstone species, this was about more than just pride. Cutthroat trout had long been a staple element in the lake's food chain and served as a portion of the diet for grizzly bears, eagles, even pelicans. Those members of the park's wildlife family were forced to adjust their eating habits to survive. As Doepke put it, lake trout "are not a replacement."

Several years into the 2000s, some $2 million annually was being invested in this all-out war. The National Park Service earmarked $1 million each year from the intake of park fees to the cause, and the Yellowstone Park Foundation, a nonprofit organization formed to supplement the costs of operating the park, donated $1 million a year as well, representing a colossal fundraising effort on that group's part. The National Park Service was also regularly aided by the East Yellowstone Chapter of Trout Unlimited, as well as the tireless physical work and the proselytizing of active member Dave Sweet.

Everyone contributes to the ability to hire gillnetting specialists from the Midwest each year; the specialists bring their boats and nets

Malachi Willis of Anchorage, Alaska, fishing on Yellowstone Lake where the regulations state every invasive lake trout caught must be killed or kept, but every native cutthroat trout must be released.

to the lake for about four or so months over the summer into the fall. That's when the lake trout pseudo-harvest reached to nearly four hundred thousand fish per season. The National Park Service was winning, but could not completely gain the upper hand. Any easing up and the remaining lake trout would reproduce at a swift rate and once again gain supremacy over the cutthroat. It was mandatory to keep the pressure on or else fall backwards. "We're deathly afraid of cutting gillnetting," said Todd Koel, the park's fisheries supervisor.

Although the commitment continued year after year, there was also no guarantee the Yellowstone Park Foundation would be able to provide $1 million in help forever. Their own officials spoke of "donor fatigue" even among the most loyal of supporters as a possible future impediment.

One angle that was still in its embryonic stage

of exploration was the development of a chemical assault of some type, a so-called poison pill that could be fed to lake trout, wiping out large numbers with comparatively minimal effort. That lies sometime in the future.

It was Doepke who noted, "Everything's on the table" when speaking of biologists' open minds in their search for answers on the late trout removal front.

The key Yellowstone on-the-scene fisheries people understood better than anyone else that it was a never-ending task to pound the lake trout in one way or another or risk setbacks. Once the fish came into the lake, it would never be 100 percent free of them again. The goal was to tip the balance back to the cutthroat so they could better thrive on their own. But they would always need some human assistance to fend off the lake trout.

"It's important we stay on it," said Pat

Bigelow, another of the National Park Service's longtime fisheries experts on the issue.

The scope of the gillnetting is remarkable. Not only do the subcontractors have their own boats on Yellowstone Lake, but the National Park Service puts some of theirs out to work, too. The nets may be stretched over thirty to thirty-five miles of water, six feet high and three hundred feet in width.

The onboard gillnetting pros get out on the water early in the day. Most tourists who see the boats from shore likely have no idea what the crews' tasks are. Much like the early automobile manufacturers, they work in assembly-line fashion, but their jobs are to efficiently raise nets, pick fish from their entanglement, and toss them aside to end their lives.

On one particular summer day aboard the *Freedom*, nine hundred feet of net were used on a shift that repeated itself from May to October.

The nets were distributed in the water and then hand-cranked onto the *Freedom*, which was named after the 9/11 terror attacks occurred. This boat did not represent freedom for lake trout, however, but perhaps a longer, healthier life for more cutthroats.

The workers needed fast fingers: when they plucked the fish, they disposed of them and those lake trout were ground to pieces. They were not stored aboard, but were transferred to containers and thrown overboard above lake trout spawning grounds. When the carcasses were heaved into the water, they sank to the bottom and suffocated freshly laid eggs identified by researchers. It sounded diabolical, the bodies of lake trout being used to kill unborn lake trout.

Dedication to removal of the lake trout was a passion for some, a job for others, but impressive all of the way around as season after season those who wished to ensure the cutthroat's fixture in

Workers hired to catch and remove invasive lake trout from Yellowstone Lake pluck the fish from nets to help the native cutthroat trout survive and thrive.

the park hierarchy put days, weeks and months into the work. In 2019, some six thousand miles of fine mesh gillnet was set in the water. Once in a great while, cutthroat trout became ensnared with the lake trout. Mostly the netting was of a size that would prevent that, but occasionally that happened. One captain said the bycatch was about five percent. If the trout was still alive it would be tossed back into the lake to swim again.

While Yellowstone Lake was the most visible front line for beefing up cutthroat trout, restoring them to their native habitat in other streams and creeks was also an aim. The National Park Service and the Wyoming Game and Fish Department had multiple programs underway for restoring what once was, but no one believed the clock would be turned back everywhere and permanently.

Through exhaustive study, collaborative meetings with the public, and judicious use of financial resources, Wyoming was doing its best under the philosophy of stewardship to identify and target lakes and streams that were practical locations for restoring cutthroat.

"It's never been the expectation we could restore them to 100 percent," said Dirk Miller, who was Wyoming's deputy chief of fisheries. "We try to balance what's realistic, and frankly, what's affordable. There are places where it's no longer viable."

Clearly, Yellowstone Lake is a part of a landscape where there is a powerful belief among inhabitants that cutthroat trout must survive as a key element in the ecosystem.

Cutthroat are a prominent feature of Yellowstone Lake. They are a prominent part of the Yellowstone Ecosystem. They are part of the psyche of the park and Wyoming. No one wants to see them disappear.

"Scientists want to make sure there are enough to sustain themselves," said Jason Burkhardt, a Wyoming fisheries biologist. "They represent the life history that was here, as well."

He pointed out that fishermen can travel many places to catch rainbow trout, brown trout, or brook trout, but they can visit only a few places to see and catch cutthroat trout. In a world where species go extinct regularly, mankind refuses to allow this one to die off.

These birds were looking for handouts of dead lake trout when the National Park Service was netting the invasive species to help preserve native cutthroat trout.

CHAPTER 18
The Invaders

The tiniest of species could wreck everything. Yellowstone National Park is in an ongoing, awareness-raising fight to preserve the cutthroat trout from an invasive species in Yellowstone Lake. But lake trout are not the only invasive species that affect the park.

Faced with invasive mussels, mollusks the size of a coin, in a small number of bodies of water in adjacent Montana and the news that walleye have threatened to take over the Buffalo Bill Reservoir on the outskirts of Cody, Wyoming, the park has acknowledged how much power carelessness or lack of a conscience could have on other waterways within its boundaries.

Simultaneously, the National Park Service and the Wyoming Game and Fish Department revved up attention on aquatic invasive species. Ramped-up boat inspections for those bringing watercraft into the state or park have brought to the fore what a serious threat to the ecosystem there could be if zebra mussels or quagga mussels slip past the workers and damage water systems.

Mussels are native to Eastern Europe, some say originating in Ukraine, but their range expanded across Western Europe attached to the hulls of shipping vessels or in the ballast water of ships, it is believed. Then they hitchhiked across the Atlantic Ocean to the United States. They were first noticed in the Great Lakes in 1988.

If mussels enter a water system, they can alter the entire ecology of the environment. They are bottom dwellers who thrive on the floor of lakes, devouring the natural plant life that feeds the native fish of that water body. Those fish run out of sustenance and, through the indirect mussels' assault on the food, can be wiped out of places where they have existed for centuries.

Although personnel wish it were so, alarms do not sound immediately when zebra or quagga mussels take hold in a lake or river. They become imbedded in mud, sand, or some plant matter, and may not be observed for quite some time.

Such an invasive species is viewed with dread as a colossal threat to fish species inside Yellowstone and on the periphery, especially on any feeder streams where cutthroat trout spawn. The arrival of mussels could undo much of the good work accomplished with removal of lake trout to rebuild the cutthroat.

It is not too strong a description to say that there is a certain paranoia level lurking inside environmental officials in case such a horrible day arrives when a treasured body of water is infected. While Wyoming and Yellowstone have emergency response programs in place to fight back, they do not want to be forced to fight at all. The amount of advance effort of preventative measures is of tremendous scope, but there is no 100 percent foolproof program to keep the waters pure forever.

The threat is minuscule in size, and carriers may be simply careless rather than evil. A few years ago the National Park Service increased its vigilance to keep the inch-sized invaders on the outside. When Montana discovered mussels in two bodies of water, the in-state reaction of Wyoming was swift and the introspection and self-examination of what might be done was intense. The topic was addressed with the hope that an invasion never happens in Yellowstone Lake, anywhere in the park, or in Wyoming.

Glacier National Park in Montana approved a policy banning boats from entering that park after the Montana findings, and Wyoming does not want to face such a scenario. "It's a disaster," said Brian Nesvik, director of Wyoming's Game and Fish Department, of the Montana situation. "It's bad stuff."

Yellowstone fisheries chief Todd Koel said the Montana discovery triggered massive attention inside Yellowstone. Wyoming's watercraft inspection stations located on main roads leading into the state feature prominent signs telling motorists hauling boats they must pull in and have their watercraft checked over. It is not only cabin cruisers or bass boats, but even kayaks come under the heading of floating items that must be reviewed by an agent.

While this may head off some problems, the stations are not staffed twenty-four hours a day and it is easy enough for someone bringing a boat into the state to avoid an inspection. A boat owner can be turned back at the border and refused entry to the state if his boat flunks inspection. Some motorist-boaters try to elude the inspections and breeze right past the stations on the highway. If that driver is noticed and his license plate can be observed, the Wyoming Game and Fish inspection individual on site passes the information on to the state highway police. If the license plate cannot be read, a vehicle description may be radioed in. The actual term at least one inspector used for the drivers who roll down the road is "a blow-by."

The watercraft inspection stations are easily spotted. Signs are posted reading, ALL WATERCRAFT MUST BE INSPECTED. Flashing lights sometimes adorn the pullover spot. Orange traffic cones may be lined up. If a driver passes at high speed, it may be because he is not paying attention, or simply going too fast. Inspectors have been known to step out of their trucks, walk toward the road, and wave their arms as an attention-getter.

A quiz follows on where the boater is coming from, what bodies of water he has been on recently, and has he cleaned his tanks. Tanks will be opened on the spot.

"Drain. Clean. Dry," is the theme from Wyoming Game and Fish to boaters. Every drop of water should be wiped off fishing gear, boots, buckets, waders, and boats. All clothing and equipment should be cleared of mud, grass, or any clinging plant life. Dry is what comes after everything is cleaned. The process is basically the eradication of the equivalent of germs.

The outreach program tries to make people think about mussels using the phrase "Stop aquatic hitchhikers." Inspectors really want to know where a boat has been, because they know which lakes have been invaded and their attention intensifies when an angler mentions a known victimized place.

The huge Great Lakes are notorious as an example of the bad stuff, as Nesvik put it, that can result from an attack of the zebra mussels or quagga mussels. That may sound like a horror movie joke, but the impact is no joke at all. The mussels have altered the fisheries so dramatically on the Great Lakes and had ripple effects on surrounding businesses that the cost of their invasion has been estimated at between $100 billion and $137 billion. Those may be outdated figures resulting from studies and surveys that have just stopped counting.

The financial impact is so dramatic the mere casual mention of the Great Lakes' experience is sufficient to scare western entities over what they might face. The concern is very much genuine in Yellowstone. Keeping mussels out comes under the heading of preserving and protecting what's there for future generations, always a guiding principle in National Park Service operations.

With three-fourths of the park contained within Wyoming, what that state does also impacts the park; and what Yellowstone does, and what happens in it, can affect Wyoming. Many boats pass through Wyoming on the way to Yellowstone, but even in 2018 some four thousand boats were inspected before being allowed on the water at Yellowstone Lake and Lewis Lake inside the park. No known mussels muscled their way into the park.

During 2019, Wyoming Game and Fish unveiled what it called a "rapid response" plan, a multi-stage action effort if it is determined mussels have invaded a body of water. This was somewhat akin to a Homeland Security Act for mussels.

The overall ruling authority of the outdoors in Wyoming is the Game and Fish Commission, which supervises the administrative department which does the work on the ground. Beth Bear, a departmental aquatic invasive species expert, informed the commission mussels "can have a catastrophic effect" on a body of water.

The bottom line is that if mussels show up, the ecosystem they invade will be altered, often dramatically, causing financially debilitating challenges. California is spending more than $10 million a year on mussel-related issues, and Lake Erie lost 95 percent of its lake trout population due to mussels (they should have worked out some kind of transfer with Yellowstone Lake and both sides would have been happy).

Being a much less populated state than California and the Midwest states, with a population of around 580,000, Wyoming still faced a $6.9 million potential economic loss from a mussel invasion through diminished fishing, boating, and shore recreation. Bear said the state would love to staff inspection stations twenty-four hours a day—if it could afford to do so and if people wanted the jobs. Apparently, being an overnight inspector is not high on the desirability list for many potential workers.

The frightening analysis offered by Bear goes to the heart of the iffyness of a wall of protection and what can occur if the wrong boat makes it through the defenses and mussels are attached to the hull, or are in the ballast water. "All it's going to take is one," Bear said.

Wyoming's rapid response plan covered many large bodies of water within the state such as Jackson Lake, Boysen Reservoir, Flaming Gorge Reservoir, and Bighorn Lake, places where residents and visitors take vacations for boating and fishing.

The process put in place by the state if there are indications of a mussels invasion includes confirmation by two experts, followed by personnel reinforcement for containment, continued sampling, and more intensive boat inspections. It is possible there could be a false positive, but unlikely, and not very likely a resolution of the

situation would occur removing any indication of mussels present once they were confirmed.

A first-stage response over six weeks would cost the department one hundred thousand dollars. If a year of increased personnel on-site was required, the cost would bloom to almost $1 million. For just one body of water. Mussels only look benign, but the long-term cost effect of their presence in previously pristine waters would continue mounting.

The huge stakes have pushed the National Park Service to investigate any and all possible preventative tools to keep mussels out of the park and especially away from Yellowstone Lake. Cost will always be an issue, but how much can the service afford not to do? Money is often at the heart of such debates when it comes to spending federal dollars.

An intriguing new development that is

A sign explaining a demonstration of expert dogs sniffing out zebra mussels on Yellowstone Lake.

gaining support for finding the mussels is dogs. Super dogs, of sorts, can be trained to sniff out and target mussels that might otherwise be hidden to the human eye even while adhering to boat hulls.

An organization called Working Dogs for Conservation provided a Yellowstone Lake demonstration in 2019 of how these trained professionals can help. Already in place in other nations seeking out invasive species and calling them to the attention of local workers, the dogs showed their stuff over a few-day period.

Accompanied by handlers, the dogs, all of them rescue dogs with specialized training, could detect zebra and quagga mussels. The mollusks were planted on the hulls of boats, the dogs found them, and were rewarded with the chance to play with a red ball. Simple as that. The dogs were easily pleased.

The dogs were not necessarily easily found, however. The ones on display had been winnowed down from groups of thousands of prospects to the few with the capability and interest in being a working dog for conservation. While it is not difficult to imagine a dog grabbing the mussel, mouthing it, or swallowing it, the trained dog actually just detects it and points it out to the handler. Humans do the rest in terms of removing the threat.

Working Dogs for Conservation has a blunt mission statement: "We train the world's best conservation detection dogs and put them to work protecting wildlife and wild places. We do it to save the world. They do it for the love of the ball."

Pete Coppolillo, executive director of the organization, said it takes a lot of weeding out to find the right dog for this kind of task. Some thousand rescue dogs are tested for every one chosen and then the others are given up for adoption. "It's a rare dog that wants this job," he said.

Dogs are well-equipped for such a task, especially when the average person on the street thinks of police dogs being capable as bomb sniffers. In comparison, sniffing out mussels seems less risky. Coppolillo said human beings have five

million scent receptors in their noses, but dogs might have 220 million. Clearly, advantage dogs. He said dogs can detect one teaspoon of sugar in a million gallons of water. That is why mussels have scant chance against the dog's nose.

When the group set up a display and gave demonstrations on the shore of Yellowstone Lake, passersby were fascinated. Park visitors drifted over and asked what was going on. The dogs served a dual purpose, showing off their prowess but also serving as educational tools. The average citizen marveled at how the dogs operated and what their role could be in the chain of protection.

While very important at this location, sniffing out mussels was far from the sexiest of purposes these animals perform as they are deployed around the world following different types of training. Some places may employ them sniffing out illegal drugs, ammunition, or other substances. The dogs come in sub-species of specialists.

Mussels are small and sneaky and mostly when they show up in a fresh body of water, no one knows how they got there. To date, it has never been completely determined how lake trout invaded Yellowstone Lake, although exhaustive investigation indicates they were illegally released there in 1994. In 1995, the discovery of their presence was declared "a crisis." The war has been on ever since, with the National Park Service finally noting the tide has turned in favor of the cutthroat—that is with the pressure staying on the lake trout.

While programs stocking various types of fish have taken place in Wyoming waters and in the park for more than a century, recently humans have begun major efforts to reverse some elements of those programs. Studies have been made and programs undertaken to eliminate nonnative fish from various streams, creeks, and lakes and restore the native cutthroat trout to those places.

Some two thousand miles of streams in the area are dominated by brook trout. Game and Fish was seeking to find the most fertile one hundred miles of water for restocking cutthroat trout.

It takes a few years for each targeted water body

to be rid of the now-established fish, mostly through chemical poisoning, restocking of cutthroat, and then allowing them time to grow to adulthood. Wyoming Game and Fish conducted hearings to "prevent species extinction," according to one high-level fisheries official, and solicit the opinions from the public as to where cutthroat should be restocked. This is a very long-term project.

One aspect of public campaigning is very straightforward. Members of the public are repeatedly urged, in Wyoming and in Yellowstone, not to release fish of any kind. This includes telling kids they should not set free their goldfish in public waters. After all, regardless of intent, the entire lake trout problem in Yellowstone Lake began when someone put lake trout where they didn't belong. Likewise, someone did the same with walleye at the Buffalo Bill Reservoir on the Buffalo Bill Scenic Byway.

And in 2014, goldfish discovered in West Newton Lake, on the outskirts of Cody and on the way to Yellowstone, created massive problems there.

The East Yellowstone Chapter of Trout Unlimited is committed to helping the National Park Service and Game and Fish with projects and in conjunction with those agencies also undertakes its own. At a given time the group might use volunteer labor to post signs warning people it is illegal to stock fish in bodies of water. Trout Unlimited will pay to make the signs and then erect them.

In part, they read, "Illegal Fish Stocking Is a Serious Crime. Since 2010 in Wyoming, a perpetrator can be fined $10,000, be charged restitution [which could truly be costly judging from the Yellowstone Lake project], be sent to prison for a year, and lose fishing and hunting privileges for the rest of their lives."

"It's like the sportsman's death penalty," said Robert Crooks, then the president of the Cody Anglers Group, which aided in the sign project.

Environmentalist, fishing guide, and cutthroat advocate Tim Wade, a longtime figure in the Wyoming and Yellowstone fishing community, cannot identify with such lawbreakers who threaten the common good inside and outside

the park by tampering with the natural order of things.

Those who put their favorite fish where they don't belong live with an attitude of "we just want what we want and the other guys be damned," Wade said. "They are people we would call outlaws one hundred years ago. It's a different Wild West. It's an environmental disaster."

It is not known if lake trout were illegally let loose in Yellowstone Lake by someone who just wanted to be able to fish for them in that beautiful lake. It is not known if walleye were illegally set free in Buffalo Bill Reservoir by someone who did not want to travel to the Midwest to fish for them.

There is no one who wants to fish for zebra or quagga mussels, so if they invade Yellowstone National Park, or Wyoming, that will not be the motivation behind the infiltration. However, the tremendous amount of damage caused by the mussels could devastate lakes and streams, and be even more significant in terms of financial, ecological, and demoralizing harm than the other issues.

Those who do wish to see Yellowstone remain what it is for the future must be supporters of the watercraft inspection program and keep those mollusks from slipping past the acutely attentive eyes of in-park and surrounding-area inspectors.

Nobody is on the side of mussels, but how devoted boaters and anglers are to preserving mussel-free zones may determine the future of Yellowstone's waters and fish.

Zebra mussels are hardly the only invasive species that don't belong in the Yellowstone Ecosystem which can do damage. In March of 2022, officials became alarmed by a report that an angler caught a smallmouth bass in the Gardner River north of the Park.

Although it was a single fish, and it is too soon to gauge long-term significance, smallmouth bass are not native to the area and pose the same type of potential threat as lake trout do to cutthroat trout in Yellowstone Lake.

Immediately, Koel, the chief Yellowstone biologist, issued a statement ordering fishermen to kill any smallmouth bass caught within the park's boundary.

A fire truck parked on a bridge at the Grant Village Campground during the 1988 Yellowstone fires. (Credit: Jeff Henry, National Park Service)

CHAPTER 19
Wildfire

Fire. Except when it provides protective warmth from the cold, humans mostly look at fire in the forest as a natural disaster. They fear it, dread it, pray that it does no damage. The word *fire* triggers a response mechanism, the immediate desire to explore methods to douse it, to put it out.

To the average Yellowstone National Park visitor that was the image of fire, and to a large extent, it still is. However, since 1988, when the most massive and destructive fires swept through the park in its history, the viewpoint has become somewhat nuanced, a viewpoint that through education leaves room for the potential value of fire in the wilderness when lives and property are not at stake.

Fire is part of the natural order of things when it comes to woods regeneration. Not every fire is a bad fire. Nor is every fire a good fire. There may be a commitment to fight back in defense of life and property within Yellowstone's boundaries. But there is no such battle line drawn to protect every tree and bush.

Yellowstone's relationship with fire grew more complex in 1988. That year was the dividing line between the outlook that every fire was horrible and the understanding that some fire could be good for the landscape. This was hardly an overnight realization, and the largest, most dramatic, most widespread burns in park annals were at the center of gripping circumstances that affected surrounding areas, as well, and left park lovers at times believing the entire 2.2 million acres might go up in flames and be irrevocably ruined.

There has been nothing to match the fires of 1988 in Yellowstone, and those who lived through them will never forget them. The attention on the fires nationwide focused on what was happening inside Yellowstone because of its national profile, but local communities also were heavily involved as flames spread outside the park's boundaries and smoke blew through the atmosphere.

Wind carried flames in various directions, setting ablaze acreage outside the park's east side, where Pahaska Tepee, Buffalo Bill Cody's old hunting lodge and famed historical structure, was threatened. Owners received conflicting messages hour to hour, first being told they were safe from destruction and then suddenly being ordered to evacuate to save themselves and as much of the buildings and their contents as possible.

It was fifty-two miles to the city of Cody, and the Absaroka Mountains on the road between there and the park could not be seen at all, so densely shrouded in smoke as they were. Yellowstone itself burned and burned, not even its vast size protecting everyone. Some areas were under siege and saved only by dedicated firefighters. In all, some 1.4 million acres of trees and land inside and surrounding the park were destroyed by fire. The flames sometimes reached one hundred feet in height.

"It was ash every day," said Loren Grosskopf, a longtime Cody resident and public official. "There was debris falling out of the sky."

For the duration of the fire, states and the federal government aided National Park Service and Wyoming workers; in total, twenty-five thousand people were involved in seeking to contain the blazes. Damage was estimated at $120 million, a figure that would be much higher today. This was by far the worst fire threat in Yellowstone's one-hundred-fifty-year history—and at times a controversial one.

Drought conditions were rampant in the park and nearby during the early summer of

The aftermath of wildfire is not attractive, and burned trees linger on the landscape for years before there is noticeable regrowth.

1988. The dryness provided fuel once fires kicked up. The first fire that became a part of the major conflagration started on June 14 in an area called Storm Creek just north of Yellowstone's boundary. Initially, it was not recognized as a significant problem. The smallish fire spread, however, growing steadily and widening.

Before the combined efforts of all those firefighters took hold, with the cooperation of weather, some 793,000 acres of Yellowstone land burned, more than one-third, about 36 percent, of the entire park. Wildlife had nowhere to run. Animals were trapped by spreading fires and collapsing trees. Approximately three hundred to four hundred elk, bear, moose, and bison were killed outright, but the ruined habitat caused feeding problems for various species and thousands of large mammals. Moose never really recovered inside the park.

Cody was close enough to send firefighters to help but also close enough to Yellowstone for residents, especially those with respiratory illnesses such as asthma, to experience breathing issues. People were told to stay indoors. There was also an underlying fear that the fire could make itself all of the way down the Buffalo Bill Scenic Byway into town and wreck homes and businesses, although the odds were against such an eventuality. Still, it is mostly forest land between the East Entrance and the city, the same type of trees and terrain that are located in the park, so such a passing thought, at least, was logical.

"At times we contemplated what would happen if it moved down the highway," said Steve Simonton, later a prominent attorney in town, though a volunteer firefighter during the blazes. "It was, 'Holy hell, that would really be something if that happened.'"

Part of such speculation was rooted in the unpredictable nature of what was taking place

A firefighter sprays water on the Old Faithful Inn against the backdrop of an orange sky and encroaching flames. The historic structure was threatened but saved from the 1988 fires. (Credit: Jeff Henry, National Park Service)

inside the park where new fires popped up, earlier fires expanded, and the wind shifted the direction of flames.

In what came to be termed the "Summer of Fire," some fifty-one fires were counted, nine of them with origins from careless individuals, others ignited by lightning. It was a time when fire seemed to overwhelm almost everything. Yet while it may seem strange to some, portions of the park were almost always open to visitors while the firefighting took place perhaps ten miles distant. At one point, the Old Faithful Inn, though, seemed to be under direct attack and people thought the historical structure was a goner. Then the fire was turned and the inn survived.

From that first fire in mid-June, many followed; more lightning and more careless campers or hikers or tourists contributed. There was a new fire on June 30, another on July 5, another on July 9, and more new blazes on July 11 and July 20. Some of them combined with one another.

A July 22 fire followed. The July 5 fire, called the Clover-Mist Fire, grew to 412,000 acres.

Avoiding daily exposure to the Democratic National Convention, vice president and future Republican presidential nominee George H. W. Bush was on a vacation fishing trip inside Yellowstone and had to shift locations along with his outfitter. The man who became the forty-first president was never in danger from the blazes, though.

The 1988 fires were so gargantuan and received so much attention that citizens around the country who didn't know a cigarette lighter from a flamethrower formed opinions about national fire policy. From the late 1800s until 1972, the Yellowstone viewpoint was much like a city's outlook. If a fire erupted, resources were thrown into the effort to stifle it and put it out. Scientists chimed in after that, indicating fires were part of the natural cycle of forest growth and regeneration, so the rules changed. It was decided that not every fire in every corner of the park was equal and should be immediately attacked with manpower and uncountable gallons of water.

Along came these massive fires, though, and National Park Service officials were caught in a difficult place. Politicians, Yellowstone supporters, tourists, and nature lovers were convinced the National Park Service was idling and enabling the ruination of the country's best-known park and they demonstrated little tolerance for this selective firefighting. Park people were following protocol, but the optics were terrible. It appeared as if they just didn't care as thousands of lodgepole pines turned to ashes and hundreds of animals were driven from their habitat and burned to death.

President Ronald Reagan was one of the most powerful critics. He referred to the existing policy of "let it burn" as "cockamamie." The fires were magnets for television cameras, so this entire matter became a nationwide issue.

Everyone in armchairs across America, even if they were seated in Alabama or Maine, had an opinion. Generally, they were not supportive of the National Park Service or the idea of letting the fires run rampant. They compared the situation to their own neighborhoods or homes. They knew if a fire broke out at their place or across the street, they wanted the fire department to respond pronto, with all it had, to put it out.

The air became hazier, the smoke thicker, and it became difficult to breathe in fouled air in communities in Wyoming and Montana on the outskirts of Yellowstone. The park is so large some people who set up camp sites were not particularly bothered and didn't feel they even had to relocate tents, never mind retreat from Yellowstone—until the wind changed and frightened them by stirring small fires into big fires and enlarging what were already big fires into huge fires.

Gradually, tourists began changing their summer vacation plans and abandoning hotel

A Yellowstone ranger gazes at a smoke column at Canyon Junction during the fires that burned 793,000 acres in the park. (Credit: Jeff Henry, National Park Service)

reservations in gateway communities. Business was dramatically affected and in Wyoming, where Yellowstone attendance can make or break a year's profits, letters began flooding into the offices of US senators Alan K. Simpson and Malcolm Wallop. The consensus of their mail was to get those National Park Service dummies more fire engines and get on their case to put the darned fires out. Wallop, especially, was a severe critic of the park's leadership, and the National Park Service.

Although he was peppered with barbs, then-Yellowstone Superintendent Bob Barbee always believed he took the right stance and even twenty-five years later defended the National Park Service's approach to combating the blazes. It was not just the policy in place, but the reality on the ground—winds dictated more of what happened and how the fires could be fought than anything written on paper, he said.

People did lose cabins and vacation homes and houses if they lived full-time in the forests on the outskirts of the park. Other places were threatened by stunning walls of flame that rose up from the ground like tidal waves. The big flames that approached Pahaska Tepee were thought to reach two hundred feet into the air and moved with stunning speed.

At the time, Pahaska Tepee owner Bob Coe was under the impression the fires approaching were three days away. Only it suddenly became apparent they were only two drainages away and closing fast. He called for reinforcements for himself, family, and employees to salvage as much of the historic site as possible. "It was pretty spooky," Coe said. "You could feel the heat and hear it. It was pretty frightening." One of his employees told the local newspaper she had never packed so fast. Another worker at the site used garbage bags as suitcases to load her clothing.

This supposedly somewhat distant blaze encroached to within one hundred yards, Coe said, and he thought everything would be lost. But the fire suddenly halted because of a change of wind and the structures were saved, not as much due to the strong efforts of firefighters,

but more so because of nature once again. From being on the verge of becoming engulfed, to a close-call escape, the fire spared him, the twenty-five people on site, and the buildings, though it took a few days before Coe felt secure enough to believe they were going to be okay.

It seemed almost by luck which cabins roasted and which were bypassed by fire. Some area residents lost longtime family hideaways and some were stunned their wooden cabins had not been devoured by flame. That was some of the unpredictable nature.

Tempers grew almost as hot as the fire itself in some quarters. Irate residents, disgusted with the "let it burn" policy, fired off strongly worded letters to the editor of the *Cody Enterprise* and other newspapers, even in one case suggesting National Park Service leadership should be prosecuted for "negligent arson."

Hunting guides and outdoor outfitters were so disheartened by the tremendous number of blackened trees and the fallen forest area they predicted the blazes would put an end to their livelihood and way of life. That did not occur, but the sheer volume of torched trees made them think so.

At the same time, those who lived in a fifty-mile radius could not resist the temptation to drive close enough to see flames with their own eyes, not merely relying on newspaper words and photographs and television images. Although most of those people did not enter the park, their day trips turned into family outings so they could act as eyewitnesses to the devastation, at least near Yellowstone and within sight of the high flames inside the park.

Remarkably, despite all of the labor used to attempt to quell flames, no firefighter was killed by the fires in 1988. There were minor burns and injuries, but no fatalities. The signature Old Faithful Inn was preserved, but sixty-seven buildings inside Yellowstone were razed by the fires.

The appearance from the air, from up close, and for a long time afterwards was compelling and horrific: seas of trees snuffed out, burnt black, turned into kindling, lying on the ground in casual piles. The National Park Service adopted the stance that it did everything that could have been done to stop the spread of the fires within its guiding rules. Many individuals were furious and did not have any interest in listening to what they considered to be rationalizations. The politics were against the National Park Service, especially in terms of the debris that could be viewed by the naked eye.

Cody Enterprise editor Bruce McCormack penned a stinging editorial, not buying the arguments made by National Park Service leaders. In part, he wrote, "We absolutely reject the notion that the park service did everything possible along the way to fight the fires. The policy was fatally flawed. The National Park Service displayed an appalling lack of flexibility and creativity."

The fires raged through June, July, and beyond August. It became apparent no matter how many firefighters were flown in and how much water was poured on the blazes in such dry conditions, they would not be easy to douse completely.

"Everybody was praying for snow," said Marge Wilder, a member of a long-entrenched Wyoming family that did lose a cabin.

Snow is rare outside the park in September, but at higher elevations inside the borders, it was entirely possible snowfall might come and do the job that even such a volume of manpower could not. And that is what happened. The sudden arrival of snow caused celebrations and an end to the wildfire ordeal in early September. Precipitation was man's secret weapon, his best ally.

The last firefighting activity took place on October 17. By the end of that month tourists began returning in record numbers. They had to dodge fallen trees and may not have relished the smell of burnt wood in so many places, but the park was still the park. The visitors were able to view wildlife that was responding to the return of normalcy for its own existence and to see up close what the wildfires wrought.

Illustrating what scientists believe, signs of recovery began almost immediately. Trees began their slow-growth process, which would take

Wildfires burned 793,000 acres of 2.2 million-acre Yellowstone National Park in 1988, the largest ever forest fire to have scorched the park. The sign in front of these trees points out how they regenerated after the fires, though it took decades.

many years to reach a peak, and nearly thirty-five years later there are some roadside signs explaining that certain trees they are gazing upon have grown in that place since the 1988 fires.

Fire policy did change after the effects of the Summer of Fire were studied, with new rules implemented in 1992 and then altered again in 2004. Some wildfires are still allowed to burn at will, but size is taken into consideration, as well as any risk to people and structures.

While 1988 is the all-time high mark for acres burned by fire in Yellowstone, some summer fire seasons since have seen very few fires with hardly any damage. Only once since 1988 has there been a significant fire season of major note that brought reminders of that milestone year, though the politics were different.

This charred piece of a tree was burned in the 2016 Yellowstone wildfires, surprising fire experts because the area had previously burned in 1988 and they did not expect a recurrence in the same area.

In 2016, some twenty-two fires, amounting to sixty-two thousand acres burned, affected Yellowstone over the summer season ending in September. This is the second largest total on record behind 1988. Once again, snow was necessary to completely contain all of the fires.

It was routinely stated by officials over the duration of the burns that "fire is part of the natural environment. Fire is part of the ecology." Three decades years later, the philosophy that nature can run wild with fire as part of the course of forest evolution had been ingrained in peoples' minds in much the opposite manner of what people understood in 1988. Environmentalists and conservationists seemed to get it.

As long as no one was dying, as long as Old Faithful, the Lake Hotel, and other buildings stood, the attitude of "let the forest burn in the distance" seemed to prevail.

This bison seems to have a very large hat size.

CHAPTER 20
Bison Comeback

Bison are everywhere inside Yellowstone National Park. They can be seen as a sea of large animals sprawled across the Lamar Valley. Miles away they may be roaming through the wide vista of the Hayden Valley. At the same time, bison by the dozen may be moseying along next to the park's main roadway, periodically crossing the street without looking both ways, occasionally just strolling along smack in the middle of the road, creating traffic jams on both sides of the road at once. The vernacular for this scenario is "a bison jam." Just as with New York City taxi drivers, it does no good to blow the horn.

On a given day an active driver touring Yellowstone might see a thousand bison, or roughly that many, though it may seem like more. They keep mounting up as a car cruises around one curve, climbs one hill, pauses next to wide-open space. This is where bison play. It can be an impressive day's viewing seeing hundreds of the huge beasts with their brown coats and massive heads together, likely the most anyone will see anywhere in the United States on the same day, or on any other day.

It is still worth remembering that these buffalo represent only the tiniest fraction of a species that was nearly snuffed out by the foolishness and selfishness of mankind. Today it may be hard to imagine what the sight of millions of buffalo must have been like on the open plains. There is no question, now in the twenty-first century, that Americans appreciate the bison they have, wherever they roam. There is a consciousness that these magnificent animals were almost lost to the earth and a sense of protectiveness and even reverence for many of them, an attitude so far removed from the late 1800s when they were victims of widespread slaughter.

Tourists drawing up a bucket list for wildlife in Yellowstone tend to rate the grizzly bear (or any bear) or the gray wolf as a higher "get" than bison, but that may be a function of comparative rarity. They are not going to bump into hundreds of buffalo at one time anywhere else even if they are fortunate to see a single wolf and one or more bears.

Yet it can be argued that if a visitor from afar sees a bison, or many bison, up close (but not too close), he has seen Yellowstone at its finest. People don't generally engage in such debates, but it seems more unfathomable to picture Yellowstone National Park minus bison than it does to envision the park without bears or wolves. Again, that may be due to simple scarcity versus abundance. Still, the buffalo carry a certain cachet as representatives of the Old West, of the past, as part of a continuum, as tenuous as that hold became at its worst moments.

This viewpoint was solidified in 2016, when President Barack Obama signed a law (the National Bison Legacy Act) that designated the bison as the United States' national mammal. There really was no objection, although some sought clarification on whether or not this elevation in status in any way imperiled the eagle's standing. The answer was no, the eagle remains the country's national bird. The only other hint of protest over this knighting of the bison, so to speak, came in joking form. A congressman from Pennsylvania mentioned that perhaps he ought to be throwing his support to the groundhog since Punxsutawney Phil, from the town of the same name, is a national celebrity, used as a winter-weather-predicting gimmick every February 2. This United States representative ultimately backed the bison, even though Obama was a Democrat and he was a Republican.

This guy looks as if he could be the leader of a pack.

One thing Obama's autograph did was bring fresh nationwide attention to the bison. Before you knew it, news outlets were not only writing headlines about the animal but also providing introductory history lessons to children and those adults who didn't know the first thing about buffalo except they were once almost all killed off.

Scientists generally concur bison are the largest land animal in North America, at their maximum weighing two thousand pounds and standing up to six feet at the shoulder, though those would be more akin to the NBA centers of the species. The females, or cows, might only weigh one thousand pounds and stand four or five feet off the ground. When babies are born, mostly reddish in color before going brown, they are thirty to seventy pounds. Some might say they resemble baby goats, though not for long. The babies can be seen learning to walk, then run, in springtime, across Yellowstone, usually trailing in their mothers' shadows and protected

by a supplemental small herd for backup. Some call the bison babies born between March and May "red dogs" because of the coloration of their coats. It takes only a few months, though, before the red fades and the permanent brown color of all adult bison takes over.

Despite the pitiless assault on bison in the late nineteenth century, and the decimation of Yellowstone's population to the point of near-extinction, the comeback growth up to 5,500 or more buffalo in the park makes it the place to go to see the animals in large numbers. The fact that there was survival of a small number of bison in Yellowstone at the turn of the twentieth century also means the park is the only place in the United States where bison have lived continuously since prehistoric times. These are the pure genetic descendants of the early buffalo and those that escaped the attempt to wipe out the herds in the 1800s.

Unless a Yellowstone visitor is educated in

bison habits, there may be a bit of disingenuousness applied to the animal's disposition. They are generally calm animals, often misjudged as friendly rather than benign when they are off to the side by their lonesome. One underestimated trait buffalo possess is foot speed. To the average human, bison look like lumbering animals. But when angered or otherwise motivated they can run up to thirty-five miles per hour or so, a frightening sight more akin to a runaway train than the roadside attraction they may have been only moments earlier.

Maybe another reason bison are not regarded with fear despite their size, power, and speed is that they are not carnivorous. They don't eat people. They don't eat big platters of meat served up on the landscape. Mostly, they stand around a lot munching on grass and other indigenous plants. Being vegetarians means the bison are perceived as less of a threat if encountered close up on a trail or in the wild. This can be misleading, since they do have a tendency to lower those king-sized heads and butt anyone or anything that gets too close. The effect is more akin to a professional wrestler's body slam than a slashing and gnashing from claws or teeth that might be the work of a bear.

One of the most peculiar and humorous of bison behaviors is when they suddenly drop to the ground and roll around kicking up dust, almost like taking a dirt bath. The first reaction might be "Huh?" There are reasons. Since they do not have opposable thumbs, bison cannot scratch off mosquitoes that descend on their broad backs, or pluck out tufts of unwanted fur. The ground roll can help in both matters.

It's important to remember that though thousands of bison are tourist attractions inside Yellowstone National Park, there are buffalo in all fifty states now, and there are bison farmers providing healthy choice meats for tables. That means the bison is back. There will never be millions loose in the western states again. Those days are gone forever, but there are bison out there. They were not eradicated.

Rick Wallen, the retired longtime buffalo expert for the National Park Service in Yellowstone, applies the acronym GOAT to bison recovery. Spelled out that stands for "Greatest Of All Time." GOAT is regularly uttered in the sports world, but Wallen felt it fit the description of the buffalo's comeback.

Wallen's definition of GOAT is that it represents the number one achievement by Americans in helping engineer the recovery of a direly threatened species that was oh-so-close to extinction. "I would argue that bison qualify for GOAT status, because their recovery occurred without the benefits provided by the Endangered Species Act," Wallen said.

The Endangered Species Act was passed in 1973, and bison recovery was underway long before that. There were only twenty-three bison left in Yellowstone as the 1900s dawned, but the population had recovered by the time Obama signed the National Bison Legacy Act.

In recent years, it has been estimated there are around half a million bison in the United States, plus another 125,000 in Canada. The numbers support Wallen's thinking. A far cry from the multi-millions of bison of mid-nineteenth-century lore, but not so few as to suggest there being danger of the world running out. As a bison expert who devoted much of his career to the animal, Wallen was pleased about the institutionalizing of the National Bison Legacy Act.

When Obama signed the act, John Calvelli of the Wildlife Conservation Society expressed the thinking of many, saying, "The bison represents so much of what we stand for, from the conservation impact of zoos, to our cultural heritage, to the ecological health of our grasslands."

Somehow, though, bison would not be bison, even in Yellowstone National Park, their favorite home, without some fresh controversy. The average tourist may be starstruck upon seeing buffalo everywhere but probably knows little about bison regulations and issues affecting the animals when he isn't hanging out with his camera and the bison isn't blocking traffic.

The fact is Yellowstone bison do not live magical existences. It shocks some to learn the herd is

There are times tourists don't know which way to look given how many bison are nearby.

basically capped and that the same bison a visitor might marvel at as it steps into range of his lens might well be culled, becoming dead meat, over the winter.

Cattlemen are at the root of bison distrust and dislike. They operate on the assumption bison are going to contract brucellosis, spread it to their cows, and wipe out their ranches. Their loud voices resulted in bison regulation. In 2000, a group formed by several government agencies on different levels implemented the Interagency Bison Management Plan seeking to appease all sides. A herd size for Yellowstone was set at 3,000 to 3,500 animals. Bison that stepped outside the boundaries of the park would be fair game for hunters.

Buffalo never got the message, and the herds continued to thrive, expanding to more than five thousand animals. Sometimes over the winter hundreds of buffalo are rounded up and killed off. This is not considered to be good public

relations, and indeed many people bristled over the tourist attractions being slaughtered in the off-season.

Some Native American tribes hoped to provide a solution by asking for a transfer of free Yellowstone buffalo to their reservations where they could start and grow their own herds. This was considered somewhat tricky business, but doable on a small scale and over time. It made sense to ship buffalo to parties that wanted them rather than killing them. A procedure was adopted whereby buffalo would be gathered, herded into collection pens, and quarantined for a suitable time period. The animals were monitored and tested for brucellosis.

This did not satisfy everyone. Suddenly, in winter 2018, what then-Yellowstone superintendent Dan Wenk called "sabotage" attacks took place. Stealth invaders sneaked into the park, slipped up on bison holding facilities, and set animals free. Fences were cut open with bolt cutters by violators to effect the escape. In mid-January, fifty-two bison were let loose to return to the wild with existing herds. These bison had been set aside, quarantined, and prepared for transfer to Native American tribes in Montana.

The next month, the same type of incident occurred again, with seventy-three more bison released. National Park Service officials instituted criminal investigations. If the aim of the saboteurs was to save bison from being culled, the acts were self-defeating, Wenk said. These bison would have been rescued by shipping them to the tribes. In their place, with the process slowed by the disruption of quarantine, other bison would be sacrificed through culling to help lower the overall park population to meet the mandates of the government plan. Wenk termed the incidents "a setback for bison conservation."

Surprised by this method of tampering and sabotage at the holding pens, the National Park Service increased security. Then some protestors of the culling chained themselves to the Stephens Creek holding pens and were arrested. In court they asserted allegiance to the Wild Buffalo Defense group.

Compounding some of the controversy surrounding bison, Wenk was shoved out of his job only months ahead of his planned retirement by the administration of President Donald Trump and National Park Service higher-ups in Washington, DC. Although he never said so outright, many believed one reason Wenk was pushed out is the expansion of the Yellowstone buffalo herd and his work with the tribes to transfer more bison to partially limit culling.

However, after Wenk was replaced and retired early, the transfer of the first bison to the tribes, delayed due to the disruptions, happened in August 2019. The first fifty-five buffalo were shipped to the Fort Peck Indian Reservation under the administration of new park superintendent Cam Sholly. Sholly called the program "the culmination of years of work," and that was no exaggeration.

Sholly said he hoped the program of such transfers would not only continue, but expand.

In late 2021, Sholly was working with other tribes to steer additional bison their way, sending the buffalo to new homes for the start-up of new herds and in January 2022, some of that patience was rewarded.

Sholly presided over the transfer of another twenty-eight bison to tribal jurisdiction. That made for a total of 182 to date from Yellowstone. In turn, tribes shipped some of their recently acquired bison to other tribes, spreading the buffalo wealth. Another conservation victory, though some could not help but take note of the irony of regional Native Americans receiving their bison one hundred fifty years later than they wished.

The completion of the first transfer set the tone, and the event was met with enthusiasm and pleasure by the tribes at Fort Peck. "Yellowstone bison are important to tribes because they are the genetically pure descendants of the buffalo our ancestors lived with," said Floyd Azure, the tribal chairman.

Suddenly, during the second decade of the twenty-first century, in contrast to the dark days of the late nineteenth century, it seemed as if everyone was on the buffalo bandwagon, from the presidential administration to Native American tribes, as well as Americans and foreigners with tourist dollars.

Some visitors loved buffalo too much and were fortunate they weren't loved to death right back. Human–bison conflicts flare up from year to year inside Yellowstone—what could be termed "stupid human tricks," with people regularly seeking to place themselves at just the right angle to pose for a selfie with a bison that wanted no part of the photo op. Or the occasional individual who must have considered a buffalo to be a behemoth of a dog and sidled up to it to try to pet it. Then there were simply the accidental collisions in which a hiker walked around a bend shielded from view and was suddenly invading a bison's space.

These types of oddball incidents and accidents happened frequently enough that National Park Service workers inside Yellowstone felt they must put out fresh warnings to remind visitors wildlife was not domesticated; animals are forever wild and do not want to make friends.

A few years ago, the National Park Service began passing out sheets of colored paper at each entrance gate. The warning flyers included the message "Think Safety, Act Safely" and the phrase "Yellowstone Is a Dangerous Place." Additional wording about being careful was printed on both sides of the sheet in numerous languages, including English, Chinese, German, and Spanish. The most dramatic message, however, was an illustration—a universal language, it might be said. The picture showed a bison, head down, heaving a cartoonlike figure of a human being into the air. In other words, the person was being gored. No gore was shown, but it could be assumed the next step in the drama was the visitor being transported to a hospital.

The upgrade in the flyer from previous warning sheets included a meaner looking bison that loomed larger. The new effort was necessary because people were still getting themselves into trouble, mostly by moving within a twenty-five-yard radius of a bison. The biggest no-no, of course, was coming too close to offspring, that is, moving between a mother and a baby. That was an inevitable invitation to inflaming mama.

One can only wonder what type of conversations National Park Service officials have behind the scenes after receiving reports of some of the stunts visitors pull. During the spring of 2015, five people attempted to take selfies with bison and for their silliness in invading the animals' space, they were headbutted, suffering one degree of harm or another.

For a time this became a nationwide joke, with some chiming in that it was really a horn tossing contest these people volunteered to participate in. When the score reached 5–0 bison, the *Cody Enterprise* ran a newspaper reader poll asking for opinions on what the season's final tally might be. Would it be, 7–0, 10–0? Infinity? Or would it stay the same because people at last wised up? Rather amazingly, the total remained the same. Visitors finally understood it was not smart to sneak up close to an adult bison and try to convince it to sashay into the same frame of a picture with them.

In spring 2016, a woman was caught on video petting a very tolerant bison. This time the buffalo pretty much ignored the intrusion. Pure luck. Another passerby reported the ill-advised behavior to a ranger and the woman was lectured.

A few months later, an incident occurred

A mama bison, a baby bison, and maybe grandpa, too.

that caused considerable outrage despite the well-meaning nature of the gesture. A tourist from Quebec, accompanied by his son from Washington, DC, came upon a baby bison on its own. Because "it looked cold" they loaded it into their car "to save it."

The men thought the baby would die of exposure if they didn't help it. Instead, this act doomed it. It is against the law to interfere with wildlife, regardless of what a visitor thinks he sees and understands. Park personnel tried to re-integrate the young bison with its mother and back into the herd afterward, but as past experience had demonstrated, it was not accepted back. The poor baby bison had to be euthanized because it could not fend for itself. The driver was fined $230 and ordered to make a $500 donation to the Yellowstone Park Foundation.

Just to prove not everyone who comes to Yellowstone is in love with the buffalo, in summer 2018 a man taunted a bison in the park by teasing it, yelling at it, and beating his chest like Tarzan near the animal as traffic snarled up. It was later claimed the same man, who escaped from the scene, created havoc in Grand Teton National Park and Glacier National Park before being arrested.

In another case of National Park Service officials likely sitting around wondering just what some of the visitors were thinking, personnel anonymously designed what was called a "Wildlife Petting Chart." The chart was superimposed on a bison as if a butcher had designated certain body parts for carving up and serving. Only in this case, the visual aid to the warnings of what might happen if a buffalo was petted showed up like this: top of the head, "Nope"; lower head, "How fast are you?"; top of the back, "Think again"; stomach area, "Vacation over"; lower body, "Do you have insurance?"; rear back, "Ouch"; and rear end, "Umm, no."

The entire National Park Service philosophy was encapsulated by this graphic, which, incorporated with the warning flyers, reaffirmed the approved Yellowstone experience with buffalo: Keep your hands to yourself.

This grizzly may seem a bit on the roly-poly side, but make no mistake, it possesses great power in its forepaws and jaw.

CHAPTER 21
The Grizzly's Future

The eyes of the world have been on the Yellowstone National Park and the Greater Yellowstone Ecosystem grizzly bear for years. Would the bear survive and thrive or be erased from this habitat?

Grizzlies are the apex predator of North America: big, powerful, scary at times, viewed with a sense of pride and with a feeling that they are symbols of the wilderness. It was in the 1970s that the Yellowstone-area grizzly gained nationwide attention as an animal whose continued existence was endangered.

Until then, it was still permissible in some western states to hunt the grizzly, just as outdoorsmen who hunted elk and deer pursued that big game. When a count was performed and it was determined there were only about 136 grizzlies remaining in the region, the bear was classified as endangered. The idea was to give the slowly reproducing grizzly time to regenerate its numbers and to protect it from extinction in the Lower 48 states.

One way or another, going on a half-century since, the grizzly bear has been a battleground topic, its future argued over by conservation groups, state and federal government agencies, National Park Service officials, and the public. There was one main point of agreement: The Yellowstone grizzly should not be allowed to die out. It is impossible to catalogue the hours of human time invested in meetings about how to manage grizzly bears, impossible to calculate the hours poured into studies monitoring the health of the population.

It is also difficult to establish just how much time has been spent in courtrooms seeking satisfactory resolutions trying to make everyone happy with the policies. Since this has never occurred, the hours keep mounting. No resolution or agreement has been produced as the years go by.

As of the early 2020s, the grizzly bear lives on within the boundaries of Yellowstone National Park and on the perimeter, a majestic mammal admired by tourists who love their snapshots of the large, furry, potentially dangerous creatures. The bears exist in quasi-harmony with mankind. It is wise for any human to be wary and take precautions in bear country, and cattle and other innocent bystander animals do become casualties. The most unfortunate people are attacked by bears, sometimes injured and hospitalized, sometimes killed. Other times close calls are registered. Wyoming and Yellowstone represent bear country, and awareness is mandatory.

What a conservation war this is, with Yellowstone National Park at ground zero of the conflict. Inside the park, the grizzly is a popular tourist attraction. Outside the park, the grizzly could be fair game at times for hunters, if they were permitted to have a season.

To even hold such a discussion, the grizzly would have to be removed from the endangered species list and declared a recovered species. This has been an ongoing, lengthy debate with dueling statistics and arguments over the best way to count bears in the wild and what numbers should be believed. Some scientists said the grizzly bear was the most studied species in the history of the world, and since the work hasn't concluded yet, they are possibly right.

By the 2000s, it was agreed the population of grizzly bears had rebounded dramatically from the low point of 136 in the early 1970s, and over the next fifteen or so years the estimate of the number of grizzlies in the Yellowstone Ecosystem expanded to more than seven hundred. That was an official measure, though rangers and Wyoming Game and Fish employees on the ground said that was a very conservative count and there were more likely 1,000 to 1,200 bears roaming the region. They based that on another counting system, plus visual evidence of bears expanding their feeding areas into ranges they had never been seen in before.

The US Fish and Wildlife Service did declare the grizzly to be a recovered species and said the adaptable animal ate everything and anything and was in no danger of running out of edibles. A court case in 2007 overturned that decision. The court wanted more hard evidence that bears had plenty to eat, since one staple of their diet had been decimated. The bears had once heavily relied on whitebark pine nuts, but a beetle infestation had been killing those forests.

It turned out that bears fell in love with a new source of nutrition—army cutworm moths. The bears expanded east to the mountains, well out of Yellowstone National Park, when the moths moved into that area. Watching in awe, scientists saw bears act like steam shovels, scooping up paws full of moths and inhaling them. They could eat as many as forty thousand moths during a session, at one calorie apiece. For the bears, it was if they had a never-ending supply of M&Ms at their disposal, a new food source, at least from mid-July to mid-September. "Who needs whitebark pine nuts?" was essentially what they were declaring.

The bears expanded their territory, which often meant they overlapped with humans in settled communities of Wyoming where they had not previously been guests. They may have been on their way to or from the moths and come across a ranch, where cattle looked ripe for the plucking as a special treat of a meal.

It became a regular occurrence for Wyoming Game and Fish personnel to be called in to deal with the problem. In some cases, a bear that had proven troublesome and killed cattle or menaced people was euthanized. In many other instances, the bears were relocated to other parts of the state,

many of those places right up next to the boundary of Yellowstone in hopes they would peacefully resettle inside the park. With luck those bears would never be heard from again as they pursued lives in the woods away from interaction with people. Or they would engage in mischief, threaten people, cross the border again, beat up on cows, get tranquilized, and then finally be euthanized for what were perceived as menacing actions and repeat offenses.

Under the operating rules, Wyoming Game and Fish was required to report to the public when a bear was captured, moved, or put down. Periodically, it seemed, the announcements came at a furious rate, a few times in a week, so swiftly sometimes it wasn't even 100 percent clear if the same bear, or another, was being talked about. At other periods of time there would be a lull with no bear activity, or at least none that required specific human attention.

There was a pro-hunting faction that pointed to the widespread human-bear encounters and argued that indicated the population needed to be controlled. Fans of bears, who preferred bears be left alone for wildlife watching, sometimes contended every bear was worth one hundred thousand dollars in visitor money simply by being available to photograph.

For residents of Wyoming especially, where more bears resided and where there were more conflicts than the other Yellowstone border states of Montana or Idaho, bears were a seemingly ever-present and never-ending issue. Grizzlies were discussion topics for years in front of government and quasi-governmental committees, with conservation groups, Native American tribes, even those from hundreds if not thousands of miles away from the Greater Yellowstone Ecosystem, chiming in.

Tourists, faraway officials, and occasional visitors seemed to feel most strongly about bears being untouchable. Those who lived in proximity, who experienced encounters up close and sometimes very personal, seemed to look at bears with a more wary eye. They also believed more strongly the grizzly bear was a recovered species

Grizzly bears are an unending source of fascination inside Yellowstone but require wary keep-your-distance approaches by humans.

and should be delisted from Endangered Species Act protection.

Many were hunters who were in the field annually for other species, elk or deer, seeking to take home meat for the freezer. They found themselves either under attack from a bear or being threatened by one. Except for residents of Jackson Hole, citizens in most cities around Wyoming supported the concept of state Game and Fish management of the animals, including using hunting as a tool to check population growth.

These, of course, were not Yellowstone National Park bears, per se. There is no hunting in the park. But they might be bears that crossed the boundaries back and forth between the national park and the state line into other management areas.

In 2016, the US Fish and Wildlife Service again recommended delisting the grizzly from federal protection. Committees representing all manner of state and federal government entities met regularly to provide reports and make recommendations on how the states should best manage the animals.

During a meeting of the Yellowstone Ecosystem Subcommittee of the Interagency Grizzly Bear Committee in Cody in November 2016, the group voted 18–1 to approve a management strategy. The one nay vote came from Dan Wenk, then-superintendent of Yellowstone, who thought some language was ambiguous. He was very much concerned about the stability of the grizzly population, very conscious that these might be his bears (as in Yellowstone bears), under his general protection, being put at risk.

After that, the Fish and Wildlife Service did something some people never expected—the agency declared the grizzly recovered and returned management of the Greater Yellowstone Ecosystem bear to the states of Wyoming, Montana, and Idaho as of July 31, 2017.

Once the action was taken, Wyoming began formulating policy on how to monitor the bears and manage the population. One element approved was a format for conducting a grizzly hunting season based on grizzly numbers and habitat, including rules about not taking females (and thus hindering reproduction).

If there was any doubt about interest in a grizzly hunt, that was promptly answered when seven thousand applications poured in for a drawing for tags. No more than twenty-two tags were available for a hunt in September 2018, which would be the first authorized such bear hunt in forty-four years.

In competition for eleven potential available licenses in one region, 3,500 Wyoming residents and more than 2,300 nonresidents paid fees of up to six thousand dollars to be considered. For those seeking a different group of eleven licenses, nearly one thousand residents and more than five hundred non-residents applied. Some anti-hunters put in for the tags in hopes of clogging up space and preventing the maximum number of bears from being hunted.

In the end, the planned hunt was suspended because a mix of conservation group allies filed several lawsuits and a Montana-based federal court reversed the Fish and Wildlife Service decision to delist, sending the matter back to the same agency and taking the jurisdiction for bear management away from the states once again.

The matter has stagnated again with

The Grizzly & Wolf Discovery Center in West Yellowstone, Montana, home of the West Entrance to Yellowstone National Park, makes a point of demonstrating grizzly bear power by displaying containers that failed to protect food for campers when bears weighed in with their strength.

Another loser in the "build a better bear protection container" sweepstakes.

resolution by the agency, the courts, and the states seemingly as elusive as ever, though there never was a time the bears inside of Yellowstone National Park lacked protection under National Park Service jurisdiction.

The park world and the perimeter world are actually two very different entities, although at times there are agreements on what the right thing to do is. Given the frequency of human-bear conflicts, Dusty Lasseter, a bear expert with Wyoming Game and Fish, sought grants and then contributions over a period of several years to obtain one hundred cans of bear spray and

handed them out to hunters for free. The gesture emphasized that bears were out there and could be dangerous.

A private company operating inside Yellowstone obtained a concessionaire's contract to set up a stand at the Canyon Village business area and rent bear spray to hikers for their protection. That proved popular with tourists.

Bears may be tourist attractions, almost part of the scenery in Yellowstone, but they do not know it is their job to be photogenic. Awareness of bears is imperative, and sometimes bear spray can be a lifesaver.

Besides periodic deaths from grizzly–human contact, there are violent interactions which individuals barely survive. Coping with a surprise assault from claws and teeth is partially a matter of instinct, partially reaction and response, and some basic luck. How badly does the bear wish to hurt you, or does he just want to scare you?

In 2009, a man walking through tall sagebrush in the small community of Clark, Wyoming, accidentally alarmed a grizzly mom and her three cubs.

This was a veteran of the outdoors carrying a handgun. The bear moved so swiftly he could not pull out his gun and could only cover up and pray for the best outcome. The man survived but was severely injured. The bear bit him in the face and crushed his jaw "like a handful of walnuts," he said gruesomely. The grizzly also lifted him off the ground and shook him like a rag doll.

Seemingly losing consciousness, the man was convinced he was going to die. "I saw a bright, white light and felt at peace with the idea," he said. "I was floating with no pain or fear." But he regained his equilibrium, picked up his rifle, shot the bear three times and killed it.

Often, a person's will can make the difference between life and death. On other occasions, such aggressive retaliation pays off when a bear loses interest, or believes a person has been neutralized and no longer is a threat to the cubs.

Hikers are urged to carry bear spray if they are not packing artillery (not allowed inside the park, but permitted in the vicinity) and are told not to go into the wild alone. Strategy for preservation against grizzly bears can vary. First is recognizing whether a charge is a bluff or serious business. People are encouraged to make noise and wave their arms to try to appear larger than they are. A sixty-three-year-old experienced backpacker from Billings, Montana, was killed by a bear in the park in 2015. He was not carrying bear spray. When his body was discovered, it was hidden under pine needles and dirt. This is an indication a bear stashed the body for future meals. Those investigating the death said it seemed this man tried to fight back but was simply overpowered by a much stronger creature.

Sometimes a casual hiker walking a dog will find his pet has been no help in an encounter, with careless barking and running about leading the bear right up to him, though sometimes the dog can act as a counter weapon. One Wyoming teacher told of a grizzly bear taking a swipe at his dog in a 2010 meet-up, but just missing the dog while the man unleashed a spurt of bear spray. Unfortunately for this man, the wind blew the spray back into his face, partially blinding him as the bear rushed in yet again. Another spray of the bear finally drove it away. It is not clear if that is a testimonial to the product or not, given how determined the bear seemed.

"I couldn't believe how calm I was," the man said. If he had dropped the can, or run out of spray, "I would have been toast."

In 2015, a man from Wapiti, Wyoming, was approached by three bears. Nationally, the incident was reported as an attack. The man, someone who had studied bear behavior, took it as a charge, not an attack, since employing bear spray drove the animals away without any truly dangerous contact.

This man was also basically unfazed by the nearness of the bears. He was searching on horseback for shed antlers in uninhabited territory, so he was not surprised by the grizzlies checking him out. "If you use the outdoors, that's going to happen," he said.

In fall 2017 a hunting guide from Powell, Wyoming, was field dressing an elk shot by a Georgia client just before dusk in the Absaroka Mountains at nine thousand feet. As guide Jon Sheets wielded his knife, the sun set and a grizzly surged out of the darkness to attack him and his client, severely injuring both as it stole the carcass. In the middle of battling the hungry bear, Sheets managed to plunge the seven-inch blade into the beast, but it did not do much damage and the animal was barely slowed.

"His ears were pinned back and he was coming hard," Sheets said.

Both Sheets and the client were hospitalized and treated for serious wounds. The bear escaped with the dead elk and could not be found and identified by Game and Fish investigators.

At the time, Sheets was in his late forties. His right ear was nearly torn off, his left elbow crushed, and bite and claw marks were imprinted on his back and shoulders. He endured multiple surgeries, was left with several scars, was out of work for many months, and was slow to completely recover.

Despite the ordeal, Sheets was thankful to be alive, able to be a family man with his wife and young son and return to the guide profession. Acknowledging he was lucky to survive, Sheets did say if Wyoming ever instituted a grizzly hunting season he wanted a crack at revenge, if not with this particular bear, then any one, as payback.

Dan White, a Wyoming senior citizen who is a bow hunter, once said he spent probably one thousand days in the wilderness and brought out his bear spray perhaps five times. Only once did he press the trigger. A bear came running at him and White tumbled backwards. On his back he reached up with the can as the bear loomed over him and fired off the trigger, propelling the pepper down the grizzly's throat. "I saw the mouth turn orange," White said.

Nic Patrick, a man in his sixties, was attacked by a grizzly bear in 2013 while walking on his own property in Wyoming and was injured in several places; he incurred bites on his face, back, knee, and hand. He said he went through several emotional stages, including being angry, though he said he was madder at himself for not having bear spray along than he was at the bear for assaulting him.

Over time, Patrick's anger subsided completely. He said he believes grizzly bears are important symbols of the region, of Wyoming, and the wild. "I love grizzly bears," Patrick said.

"I always have and I always will. The grizzly is the poster child. They are a fit for the landscape. There are very few places like this. We have wild country that supports animals that were here two hundred years ago."

And the area has Yellowstone National Park to spotlight them.

Grizzlies are important symbols of the region, of Wyoming, and of the wild.

On any given clear day, visitors to Yellowstone may be blessed with a gorgeous sunset.

CHAPTER 22
Yellowstone Always Yellowstone

They come from all over. Yellowstone National Park may be surrounded by residents of Wyoming, Montana, and to a lesser extent Idaho, but on a given day in the summer a visitor who is on the lookout might see license plates from almost every state in the country.

It may be an all-day driving project, with many miles covered, but people have been known to count license plates representing just about all of the states (good luck with Hawaii) and perhaps every Canadian province, too. Yellowstone is such a lure that it is an equal attraction to those who live in hot and humid places in the nation's corners or those who live in similar terrain nearby.

It is more likely a citizen will drive from Alaska to Yellowstone than somehow transport a vehicle from Hawaii, and Delaware being such a small state it may be possible to miss out on spying a plate from there. Likewise, it's not clear how many Canadians drive from the Yukon Territory, the Northwest Territories, or Nunavut, especially since there are no roads from Nunavut. Still, some certainly make it there.

Tourists also come from all around the world, and only a few years ago so many thousands of visitors used their newly disposable income from China on vacations to Yellowstone that gateway communities opened more Chinese restaurants and existing ones made special arrangements with Chinese tour companies. Clearly, the trend was top-heavy with people of Chinese origin outnumbering those from other nations. The COVID-19 pandemic disrupted this trend, and at least temporarily, the disease variants continue to impact international tourism.

Annual attendance kept growing by the thousands upon thousands inside Yellowstone after 2015 as all American national parks gained

in popularity. Fans just kept on coming. Trouble, or weirdness, kept following, as well.

In 2015, while they were on trial in Canada for a terrorist plot to blow up a train traveling between Toronto and New York City, it came out that two men from Tunisia had investigated detonating an explosion in Yellowstone. They thought it would trigger a massive eruption from the below-ground super volcano. They had not figured out how to reach the magma nine miles below the earth's surface by the time they were nabbed for the other conspiracy charges. According to authorities, the men's thinking went like this about the United States: "Wouldn't it be great if my enemy's worst national disaster could happen?" Since the World Trade Center towers had been previously destroyed as symbols of American decadence, it would have been intriguing to probe the reasoning of terrorists to learn what made them think of Yellowstone as a weapon.

Rarely was one event so highly publicized and met with negative outrage as a 2016 incident. A group of young Canadians calling themselves "High On Life Sunday/Fundayz" could not resist treading upon the soft ground surrounding the Grand Prismatic Spring and its dazzling, colorful waters, and also boasted about doing so through social media.

Illegally walking across forbidden land, which could cause long-term damage, the handful of friends posted photographs of their misdeeds on Facebook, rounding up followers as they broke rules and regulations at iconic sites in Yellowstone, but also in other parks. Some seventy-five days into a trip, they tramped around the ecologically fragile grounds at the Grand Prismatic Spring and drew attention to themselves. Soon after, three members of the group were arrested and charged with multiple violations.

Yellowstone admirers and environmentalists shouted back at the violators online just as vocally, rebuking them for callousness and selfishness, bashing them for their disregard of the warning signs admonishing people to remain on pathways and to stay away from thermal areas. When the outcry reached the partners in crime, an apology was issued, but it was not warmly received. In part, the apology read, "We did not respect the protected environment we were exploring and we want to acknowledge our wrongdoing. We have realized that what we did was not okay and we want others to learn from our mistake."

Many doubted the sincerity of those who had posted film footage of their aberrant behavior. One stinging comment read, "Your narcissism is astounding. You damaged a natural wonder not to promote its majesty, but your own. I hope you are prosecuted to the fullest extent of the law."

They were. Eventually, it was discovered this was a pattern of recklessness in more than one American national park, with a trail of violations left behind at Zion National Park, Death Valley National Park, Mesa Verde National Park, and two Bureau of Land Management sites. The arrogance of bragging about the misdeeds contributed to the individuals' undoing. Members of the group served up to a week in jail and were placed on probation, fined, and banned from Yellowstone.

Some two years later two people from this same group (along with a third person) were in a park at Shannon Falls, British Columbia, fell one hundred feet, and were killed at a waterfall. Officials said they should not have been in that area in the first place.

Most foreign visitors view Yellowstone as a

While grizzlies receive more of the attention, some extra-large black bears roam the backcountry in Yellowstone National Park, too.

remarkable place of scenic beauty and they are drawn, as if magnetically, to visit as part of their tours of the American West. They arrive with curiosity and depart with reverence.

A one-time mayor of Cody, Wyoming, Nancy Tia Brown, said, "We think of it as ours, but I think it's an international icon."

Yellowstone means different things to different people. For some who arrive in a van after driving one thousand miles from the Midwest, it is about nostalgia and taking their kids on a trip they took with their own parents. They want to see the same bears and bison and elk they saw as youngsters (if not literally the same animals). Others are most attracted by the thermal features, Old Faithful in particular. For those who live in the flatlands, they wish to see mountains and forests, and hike and camp in the wilderness in an environment nothing like their home-city neighborhoods.

Fly fishing is a bucket-list assignment for some: fishing on the famed Madison River, Yellowstone River, or the park's other streams, or bringing in a cutthroat trout on Yellowstone Lake. Yellowstone has its own fishing license fees. Buying a Montana or Wyoming state fishing license does an angler no good; he or she must still buy a park license. Much of that fee money, however, goes to funding fisheries programs in the park, including the effort to rid Yellowstone Lake of those invasive lake trout.

In many ways, one hundred fifty years later, Yellowstone is the same park as its founders in 1872 hoped it would be. There may be miscreants like the Canadians crisscrossing thermal features and doing damage, people ill-advisedly trying to pose for pictures with bison, and those intentionally breaking rules and seeking to avoid being caught. In the late 1800s and early 1900s there were fewer rules to break, and the focus on law-breaking was more heavy-duty, such as poaching.

It turned out, as pioneer ranger Harry Yount said from the start, Yellowstone really did need a police force to keep the peace, protect the landscape, and prevent criminals from gaining a foothold. Early superintendents Stephen Mather and Horace Albright may not have been right about everything—not many would advocate feeding garbage to bears these days with fans seated in bleachers—but one of their fundamental premises was correct.

They believed the more people were attracted to Yellowstone, the more people would care about the park and they would wield their influence as voters, lobbyists, or donors to support programs that in the long run offered protection to the wildlife and the wild land. To see Yellowstone was to fall in love with Yellowstone, those leaders felt, so the key to long-term sustainability was to convince more people to come and see. The more people who experienced Yellowstone—passed on the word, wrote about their time there, shared photographs of what they came across—the stronger the Yellowstone lobby would be.

This all came true. Perhaps it was inevitable the embryonic environmental movement of the early twentieth century burgeoned and spread. Multiple groups were formed, including the Sierra Club, conservationists focused on protecting wolves and other wildlife, the Rocky Mountain Elk Foundation, groups representing hunters and fishermen, and friends of various parks, especially Yellowstone and more.

One way or another, lovers of mountains and forests, rivers and waterways, bears and wolves, trout and other fish, hiking in the backcountry, family outings—all were attracted to Yellowstone. For so many, seeing Yellowstone in the flesh, so to speak, meant fulfilling a long-held desire. They had grown up hearing about the marvels of the showcase, grown up turning the pages of *National Geographic*, even though they lived 1,500 miles away, and wanted to see it with their own eyes, and bring their children to see it with their own eyes.

For some, Yellowstone is a destination. For others, stopping at the park is a drive-by, a short stop as part of a lengthy driving vacation. One family from Nebraska stopped in. Equipped with fishing rods, the clan made sure to pause and wet a line in the Yellowstone River. Dream come true to fish in Yellowstone, if only briefly, they said. The family, with kids in their early teens, was on a ten-day vacation.

"Just coming up here," said the father, "was on the bucket list. This is paradise for us. We're fishing for anything that bites. We'll take whatever it is." Then he could tell his friends he once caught a fish in Yellowstone National Park.

These folks from Nebraska were hardly among those who came the farthest to fish. For some, Yellowstone fishing is the primary reason they are there. For others, it is just one thing to do while they are in the park.

"People come from all parts of the globe . . . and appreciate it," said park fisheries expert Todd Koel.

The words "cutthroat trout" woo, but the park also offers the opportunity to catch other fish in a fabulous setting. That brings people to the shores of the rivers and lakes. The scenery is not to be underestimated. "It's hard to beat," said one man from Las Vegas on his third visit to Yellowstone mainly for fishing.

An Austin, Texas, man caught a brook trout and took a picture of it with his phone. It wasn't even a large fish, but it was proof-positive of a fish captured on his trip, so others back home could see what these fish were like. "It's one of those awesome places you think about fishing," he said of Yellowstone.

One joy of Yellowstone is rounding a bend in the car, perhaps in the Lamar Valley, perhaps on the road to Cooke City, maybe climbing high to Sylvan Pass, when there, suddenly, on the road, or alongside the road on the other side, is a herd of something.

A man driving the twisting, winding road up the hill from the East Entrance to the top of the pass abruptly faced a half-dozen sheep, the rams with magnificent curls, just beyond a metal barrier fence only feet off the road. They were relaxing on a rock ledge over a canyon, so close they could almost be touched. They were also so comfortable they were disinclined to run, even after he found a place to park the car on the narrow two-lane road and hurriedly hauled out a camera.

Rams with their large curled horns are very impressive animals to view in the wild.

There they were for the posing, creatures of the wild enjoying cool morning air in the early fall, when the park was less crowded than in summer high season.

That area seemed to please the sheep. On another day, across the road, higher on a hill, only a very short distance above the traffic, picking their way across rocks, were another half-dozen. In both cases, the animals seemed to invite photographs, providing a particular opportunity, possibly due to their own laziness of the moment.

Sheep are not as easily seen as bison or deer or elk in Yellowstone, even less regularly seen, it seems, than grizzly bears. Not wolves, though. Wolves remain the ghosts of the park.

Antelope, too, make themselves scarce. They tend not to crowd the park road, are very wary, and when they bed down they seem to prefer areas just a little farther back from the highway where they have more room to run. And they can run. It is said the pronghorn antelope can reach a speed of one hundred kilometers per hour (62.5 miles per hour). If the animal wants to bound away, it may disappear at faster than Olympic speed.

Montana author John Clayton wrote Yellowstone, "as effectively as any place in the country, fulfills expectations." He also uses the word "special" almost interchangeably with Yellowstone, saying it lives up to that designation.

Mather and Albright would likely be proud of the performance of the National Park Service and the rangers who serve. They would likely also be pleased there are ranger training academies, one at the Grand Canyon named for Albright, and one at Harpers Ferry, West Virginia, named for Mather.

Many rangers are career employees devoted to the parks, with a passion for the outdoors and a lifestyle that makes them protectors of America's treasures even as they aid the millions upon millions of visitors who take the treks to see what those special set-aside places offer.

It helps to be devoted, because while park rangers can make a living as a federal employee, they are not paid as well as doctors or lawyers. A running joke in the 1920s in conversations with tourists went something like this: "How much do they pay you, ranger? It's so wonderful up here in the mountains, you ought to be willing to work for nothing." The ranger response supposedly went this way: "That's about what we do, ma'am. All we do is answer questions during the day and dance all evening with the pretty lady dudes. And to think they give us a hundred bucks for it!"

Richard Jones of Wapiti, Wyoming, was a National Park Service ranger for twenty-five years, and his father was a ranger before him. He was always struck by a book titled *Islands of Hope* by Phillip Manning, and said, "That's one of my favorite phrases about the park service. We have so many great things that could be lost so easily."

Rangers like Jones, it might be said, are the first line of defense and the last line of defense; they protect the national park resources from litterbugs and the reckless who won't follow rules, while they are also pressed into action fighting fires and helping the environment hold fast against natural world or human erosion.

Jones offered the unique perspective that Yellowstone, and the other national parks, are really museums housing those artifacts so future generations, some yet unborn, can come to see them.

"These are just big museums," Jones said of the parks and giving them proper respect. "You don't roller skate in a museum. You don't fly a kite in a museum. There are a million other areas where you can go for that."

The famous Grand Prismatic Spring is probably the most colorful water in North America.

CHAPTER 23
The People Still Care

Proving that the creation of Yellowstone as the world's first national park in 1872 was an inspired idea some one hundred fifty years ago, people enjoy, love, and protect the iconic landscape more than ever.

Rather than needing the endorsements and public support of superintendents Stephen Mather and Horace Albright to convince Americans to visit Yellowstone, after a century and a half as the beacon of a fresh and widely embraced concept, current and recent superintendents are tasked with worrying about too many people coming to visit the park's 2.2 million acres at the same time.

While those early leaders favored such gimmicks as feeding grizzly bears in front of an audience to spread word-of-mouth reasons to come on in, modern leaders ponder how to spread the enthusiasm over longer time periods, or at least efficiently move people between valleys and waterfalls, thermal features and bison congregations.

Their concern is that after all of this time of living up to the mission to preserve Yellowstone for future generations, those generations will miss out due to damage from overuse and overcrowding. More than anything, they do not want Yellowstone to be loved to death.

Before such threats become reality, they are wrestling with the questions. Issues in Yellowstone include (like everywhere else) climate change; fighting the invasive lake trout in Yellowstone Lake; coping with crowds on the roads at the height of the summer season; the future of grizzly bear management in the region; ripple effects from the reintroduction of the gray wolf; and the prolific reproductive nature of the healthy bison herds.

These are things that make Yellowstone *Yellowstone* and are all aspects of park life that are of major concern to visitors and supporters of national parks.

Mather and Albright would be pleased how people have become so devoted to Yellowstone. In the earliest days of the park's existence, when Nathaniel Langford was an unpaid superintendent with no staff, it seemed the only ones entering the park's boundaries were explorers or poachers. Now Yellowstone National Park is a bucket list destination for millions of Americans, and foreigners, too.

By the end of 2021, the rough total of visitors Yellowstone hosted since 1872 was around 195 million and growing annually. As recently as 2000, the annual turnout was 2.8 million. Attendance first passed three million in a calendar year in 2003, but it dropped below that figure again for a few years in a row after that.

After several years of three-million-plus visitation, in spring 2015 then-deputy superintendent Steve Iobst predicted that one day in the future Yellowstone would inevitably attract four million visitors in a calendar year. It happened that year, barely six months after Iobst made what seemed like an off-hand comment. The final attendance total for 2015 was 4,097,700.

The unexpected surge caught National Park Service officials off guard. They were planning for a possible record year in 2016 to observe the one hundredth anniversary of the founding of the National Park Service. Nationwide, the Department of the Interior and national parks officials touted that special anniversary as a grand opportunity to visit the parks. At New Year's, Yellowstone's then-superintendent Dan Wenk even rode in a float in the Tournament of Roses

Parade in Pasadena, California, heralding the big year to come.

The eyes of the nation were on the anniversary and the efforts of the government were on promoting it. From that standpoint, it was a successful celebration. Yellowstone set a new record, ringing up 4,257,000 visits. From a management perspective the number was a bit worrisome. The first thoughts of how many people were too many were voiced.

This ruminating focused on whether or not the attendance would continue to rise. Reality provided a little bit of leavening. Attendance did not recede to the three millions, but in the immediate aftermath of the National Park Service anniversary visitation challenged the new record and hovered close to it, but did not exceed it. For a few years, the new normal seemed to be about four million visits.

During the waning days of the Wenk superintendency leading into the Cam Sholly administration, talk began about whether Yellowstone was going to be overrun by friendly folks. Studies were made sampling visitor experiences, asking opinions about crowding.

Planners and theorists initiated discussions about whether or not one day the automobile—which had made Yellowstone so accessible for decades—might have to be banned. Or whether some bus routes might be initiated. Or whether caps on attendance on certain days, weeks, or months would have to be instituted. There were concerns about restroom sufficiency. It was one thing for bears to, *ahem*, "go" in the woods, but not appropriate for people.

Those who made their living off Yellowstone, the restaurant owners, hoteliers, and tour guides in the gateway communities of Wyoming and Montana, were alarmed over what might transpire. Purists who believed Yellowstone was for all the people and should not be closed to anyone also worried. Others whose experiences did not match the grumpiness of visitors who felt the situation was overcrowded—except at a

Some thermal features are surrounded by colorful fields of flowers.

few locations—thought the situation was being unnecessarily exaggerated.

Indeed, one could drive for miles at the forty-five-mile-per-hour speed limit around the park without being hampered by traffic, even at midday in July, if the visitor skipped a stop at Old Faithful, or chose not to pull into a heavily visited geyser short on parking. As for bison jams, or wildlife-generated traffic crushes, that's why people came, wasn't it, to witness the wildlife?

There should have been no complaining by tourists if they got stuck in traffic because a buffalo was strolling down the road. They were presenting themselves for viewing, just what the visitor ordered. Still, in fall 2020, the National Park Service announced plans to try out a shuttle bus program; the public relations announcement contained the words "Always working to improve visitor safety, access, and experience."

One aspect of the program introduced an experimental automated shuttle bus running between Canyon Village and campgrounds, and between visitor service buildings and the local lodging facilities. Drivers to Canyon could leave their cars parked in the lot while hopping on a "low-speed" shuttle. Wave of the future? Maybe. Superintendent Sholly said it was worth knowing about the possible value of future transportation technology.

Previously, there had been mention of the establishment of shuttle buses from locations in gateway communities in place of private cars. The idea of prohibiting cars was a touchy subject, though over a few-year period National Park Service leadership said it was obligated to study alternatives in case attendance mushroomed to the five million mark at some point.

Since nearly 4.9 million people visited in 2021, that new number barrier was fast approaching and seemed likely to be surpassed in 2022 in connection with the park's one hundred fiftieth birthday or soon after.

Unlike Iobst, who was blindsided by the swift increase as visitation crossed into the four-million-plus range, Sholly was saying aloud attendance might keep growing. If it did, he felt

the responsibility to study ways to alleviate any crush, though he did not want to rush into controversial moves.

One thing proceeding apace, as any visitor to the park could tell, was road construction. Whenever a tourist enters the park and is handed the current newsletter, a portion of the newspaper explains the nature of construction, road closures, and the like. There is always some revamping going on, often more than one project simultaneously, some projects stretching across multiple seasons.

Fishing Bridge was being remade, while a road here and a road there featured twenty-minute or longer traffic delays, even without bison in the way. It was a nonstop construction effort more reminiscent of stretches of interstate highways that were supposed to make life easier for drivers, but certainly drove some locals into hiding, or at least limited their visits to prime-time shoulder seasons like May or September.

All of this proved that as much as Yellowstone was never-changing, it was also ever-changing. It was interesting when Sholly, or other National Park Service employees, reported to constituents on the results of visitor surveys that some 75 percent of first-time visitors said their experiences were positive. Perhaps they didn't know enough to complain about man-made traffic jams due to the same type of construction work they could have faced at home.

Regular and longtime visitors know the difference and might well have been driven half-crazy by the construction that added considerable travel time to different routes where they were used to breezing through certain junctions. It often seemed the construction was nonstop, and that might well even be true, with such a pattern continuing for years.

In August 2019 in a talk before a group of government officials in Cody, Wyoming, Sholly tried to put the kibosh on fears of restrictive policies taking shape for visitation, saying at the time neither a bus shuttle system from outlying communities to specific locales inside the park, nor

Where the deer—or in this case—where the antelope play.

a reservation system limiting how many people could drive in on a given day, were in the works for "the foreseeable future in any way, shape, or form."

It is not clear how that philosophy might jibe with the more recent announcement of shuttle experimentation. A reservation system, effectively keeping people out, would seem to defy the spirit of the park system and go against the grain of the always-welcoming atmosphere throughout the years.

Of course, situations do arise when it is wise to ban certain individuals from Yellowstone because of their behavior, such as those Canadians who marched all over the ground near the Grand Prismatic Spring. In fact, when some people charged with crimes or violations of park rules are hauled into the court inside Yellowstone, there are times when penalties include banishment from this park and all national parks.

There is such a thing called national parks etiquette. Mostly the rules revolve around common sense and respecting the resource. Do not approach wildlife, for your own benefit and theirs; adhere to the advice of rangers; and follow the basic regulations, often explained on posted signs. Mostly this means to stay on board-walk paths rather than stepping off into fragile territory. Visitors are injured because they do not stay on the straight and narrow.

In recent years, many times a visitor curious about stepping onto a thermal feature has been warned not to do so for their own good by a nearby fellow tourist. Other times tourists wielding camera phones record violators' stunts and report them to the authorities.

It is estimated 90 percent of Yellowstone visitors never venture more than a mile from Grand Loop Road, so they are more often in proximity with one another than with wild creatures in the backcountry. The backcountry, away from lodges, campgrounds, roads, restaurants, and stores, is where solitude can be found. That is also where campfires can ignite forest fires through carelessness. The sentiment behind the phrase "It takes a village to raise a child" also applies to treatment of national parks. The features and resources must be cared for by the many who share the responsibility of preservation, not only the uniformed officials.

Yellowstone stands out, and anything that happens within the park seems to gain more attention nationwide than when something happens in another park. Neighboring Grand Teton is sort of a twin national park, or at least a sibling, with much of the same terrain and wildlife, and it is situated right down the street. Yet Yellowstone, perhaps because of its fame, seems to attract more of the zany.

Still, in 2019, Grand Teton had to close its Signal Mountain Summit Road for a time because visitors were feeding bears. As a textbook case of why humans should not feed the animals people eats, the bears got so worked up they began making bluff charges at park personnel and other visitors, likely in hopes of obtaining extra goodies.

The National Park Service seems forever to be lecturing the public on the do-nots of behavior. One behavior encouraged a few years ago was telling people to honk their car horns to scare away bears that might approach. This one suggestion was probably completely ignored. A main reason visitors come to Yellowstone is to see bears, so if one appeared out of the trees, the tourist's first thought would not be to scare it away.

Yellowstone was not about to relinquish its title of attracting the most crazy people easily. In September 2019, two men walked up to the rim of Old Faithful (between eruptions) in order to snap close-up photographs, but the trespassers were immediately apprehended by park rangers.

While their behavior was foolish and risky, they did not seem to match the disrespect shown by a man who was viewed pulling down his pants and urinating into the cone of Old Faithful. The law-abiding, camera-savvy onlookers were aghast and also provided information to rangers.

It wasn't long after the duo peering into the rim of Old Faithful were nabbed that another man decided to take a walk near the iconic park feature, fell into a thermal pool, and seriously burned himself. He was apparently drunk at the time. The middle-aged man had basically completed his trek in the dark and was trying to return to the Old Faithful Inn when he fell.

The man somehow made it back to his room before realizing how badly he was hurt, then called for help. He was subsequently transferred to a burn center for treatment in Idaho Falls. Searching rangers found a shoe, a hat, and footprints on soft ground near the geyser's cone. Officials said the typical water temperature where the man tumbled is between 150 and 200 degrees Fahrenheit.

Thermal features are beautiful objects of intrigue, but they can also be dangerous. The park's website has a warning message that reads, "Hot springs have injured or killed more people in Yellowstone than any other natural feature. Keep your children close and don't let them run."

Yellowstone seems to be investing in more professional studies about people, animal, or climate behavior in recent years. The National Park Service is always studying something. Materializing as a report, one study came out in late 2019 on how frequently the appearance of bears near roads caused traffic jams. A total of 240 bear jams were counted based on reports. Park bear biologist Kerry Gunther speculated that with more people showing up, it seemed logical bears will become more habituated to humans and there might be even more jams. It would not be a good thing, however, if the increasing number of people resulted in more confrontations between bears and humans, more injuries to humans, and more deaths of bears from being put down.

Somehow bears always work their way into Yellowstone conversation. Did you see a bear? That is a common query of a visitor. How close was the bear? Do you think grizzly bears are a recovered species in the Yellowstone Ecosystem? Do you think Wyoming will ever hunt bears again? Bears are always a subject of fascination—their visibility, their nearness, their status.

One way the enduring fascination and appreciation of Yellowstone National Park is measured, of course, is that simple statistical count of just how many people come to see its splendor.

Excepting war years—World War I and World War II—it can easily be argued that 2020 was one of the worst, if not *the* worst, year in the history of the United States. The nation was fully or partially paralyzed for month after month by the COVID-19 pandemic. The coronavirus forced Americans to stay at home, to forgo travel. Businesses were shuttered. The travel industry

This red fox is on its own looking for its next meal.

collapsed. No part of the country or the economy was immune.

That included the National Park Service and the National Parks System. All entities were shut and monitored. Yellowstone follows a rolling schedule of openings at its five entrances each spring, beginning in April and going onward into May. When the calendar reached those days, the park remained shut as the country and government deliberated the proper protocols. Yellowstone was closed outright between March 24, 2020, and May 18, 2020.

Beginning in mid-May and continuing through June 1, at different entrances, Yellowstone tentatively opened for business, allowing in visitors with restrictions. Staff members and concession workers faced rigorous testing and social distancing requirements, and the positive test rate was amazingly low week after week.

Many people may have been hesitant to visit the park initially, but as time passed and states'

restrictions eased, more and more tourists felt the tug of the wide open spaces and the desire to get out of the house and visit a famed American institution. Yellowstone, it could be reasoned, was dominated by the kind of space that made it easy to social distance and stay clear of others. You could move about within the confines of your automobile and stop wherever you wanted, and you didn't have to crowd together with others.

Visitors tended to wear face masks in the busiest of areas, such as Old Faithful, but did not do so when simply stepping out of their cars to gaze upon scenic areas or bison, bears, and elk in their habitat.

The early returns were slow, but by July, annually the most crowded of times for Yellowstone, visitation numbers were rapidly climbing. It was obvious something was going on that seemed unusual. The official tourist count for the month was two percent higher than it had been in July 2019, when the country was not threatened by a pandemic or anything out of the norm. Some 955,645 people came to the park in July 2020.

This became a trend. In August, the same pattern followed. That month attracted 820,000 people, an increase of 7.5 percent over August 2019. This was the second busiest August ever recorded at Yellowstone.

Usually, attendance begins to slip as fall beckons. Students return to school, so families complete their summer vacations by then. Also, the temperatures at higher elevations cool and Yellowstone can both get nippy overnight and receive snowfall. However, the results astounded many. Even as the nation debated the proper procedures for sending children back to school, even as professional sports teams and college football teams were scaling back or eliminating spectators, people poured into Yellowstone.

During the month of September 2020, some 837,000 visits were recorded at Yellowstone. That was an increase of 21.6 percent over September 2019 and set an all-time record for visitation during that month. The previous record of 724,000 people was established in September 2018, and the 2020 mark was 15.6 percent higher.

The same was true for October, a month historically far less busy. But word spread that pandemic or not, people could recreate in Yellowstone without fear of inhaling anything besides good, clean air. Once again the National Park Service catalogued remarkable statistics on visitation for the month.

As the calendar flipped to November, the total for October 2020 visitation reached 360,034, a jump of 110 percent over October 2019. It also became the busiest October ever; the old record of 252,013 visitors totaled in 2015 was some 43 percent less.

And all of that was without the participation of major tour bus companies that heavily influence total attendance when they bring in thousands upon thousands of people each year, many of them foreign tourists.

It should be noted that next-door neighbor Grand Teton also set a September record in 2020 with 603,000 visits, up 17 percent over the previous September.

Much like the early 2000s, when the United States felt under siege because of terrorist attacks and Americans sought comfort in their home country, it seemed people once again turned to Yellowstone and their national parks for solace in the face of the ongoing coronavirus outbreak that distressed the nation.

Following up on the deluge of visitors in 2020, as soon as the National Park Service invited them onto the grounds when pandemic restrictions eased up, Americans brought the same mentality to 2021. Month after month they flooded the grand park and its environs, smashing attendance records monthly. In July of that year, Yellowstone experienced its first million-person month.

For a time it seemed probable park visitation would actually top five million for the first time, but the total was shy of that new milestone, with the annual total 4.86 million. It is clear in the 2000s that the experiment of 1872 to create a national park still meets with the American public's satisfaction.

Yellowstone National Park endures with special stature in Americans' minds at all times, but it seems to play a specifically warming, encouraging, and comforting role in times of trouble. When Americans are not taking overseas trips, they seek their roots and turn to Yellowstone, its wildness, its history, its preservation of the past, and its place as a welcoming paradise that can make them feel more at home than when they are home.

Hey gang, the food is very good here.

EPILOGUE
Yellowstone Never Gets Old

One of my favorite times in Yellowstone National Park was my visit for the first time in years during the summer of 2014 while living in Cody, Wyoming.

A thrill went through me when I saw my first buffalo of the visit by the side of the road, then the second, third, and a small herd. It was like revisiting the past, a mini glimpse of the 1800s when bison were everywhere on the plains and before the slaughter began.

They were everywhere inside Yellowstone. Some wandered on their own, soloists here and there, hunkered down on their bellies, or bending over munching grass. Many were bunched together in herds, thirty, forty, or fifty sprawled on the ground, standing still, or making as if they wanted to cross the park road to get to the other side. Why? Maybe the quality of grass or plants was better there.

Most of the huge animals looked alike, deep brown skin, patches of fur, enormous heads, some a bit more oblong than others, baleful eyes that read the situation and seemed quite confident as each move was made despite the approach of automobiles. Luckily, the cars moved on the slower side, down to twenty miles per hour or reduced to a near standstill once the bison took over with their proud strut.

Wildlife has first dibs on the roads in Yellowstone, but then few drivers want to pass them up anyway, and are inclined to slow or brake to a halt to watch them. Mostly, I chuckled when I came upon bison either blocking the road completely in a string, waltzing down the middle of the road on the yellow divider line, or just taking over completely with their attitude of indifference to the power of the automobile.

Once, I ended up stopped in the right lane in a row of cars with another auto back-up across the street and a little farther down, the bison in the middle, hanging out as if this was a personal favorite street corner. It was summer and warm out, and I had the driver's side window rolled down as I gazed upon the animals. Suddenly, I felt a breeze. Some bison sneaked up, weaving between cars, heading to a meet-up with the other buffalo. Being parked, I had not been gazing in the rear-view mirror and never saw them coming. One brushed past so closely that not only could I have stupidly petted it, it missed bumping into my arm by inches. I promptly rolled up the window.

One spring, the orangish baby bison, the fifty-pound youngsters only recently born, were all over the neighborhood. Some nuzzled their mothers, some lay conked out on the grass, indifferent to the world around them. Protective mothers remained close, and it seemed several other adult members of the herd kept a watchful eye. A friend who is a professional photographer and I watched a man who began creeping closer to the herd for better photos with his camera phone. As he edged toward the little ones, the big buffalo began edging toward him. They displayed tolerance, but we thought the guy might well be gored.

Other visitors urged him away, but the man paid no attention. If the bison charged, I suggested we rush in and save his life so we could be awarded the Carnegie "Hero" Medal. My more cynical friend said *nah*, this foolish person was on his own and he was going to snap a Pulitzer-Prize-winning picture of the man being smashed to bits. We hung back and wondered what one more step would bring. Nothing happened. The group of bison slowly moved away, and the man

Deer are always on the alert for any predator threat.

stayed put. There never was a charge, an injury, or a prize-winning photo.

It was impossible to visit Yellowstone without seeing bison. Sometimes that spoiled people, who because of the animals' proliferation seemed to take them for granted. I never tired of buffalo, remembering their place in history before man did his best to eradicate them. Part of it was habitat by association. The bison belonged here, in Yellowstone. They were home where they belonged, situated where they could thrive.

For all of that, I could never deny the excitement I felt when I came upon a grizzly bear, on a hillside, crossing flat ground, in search of food, or occasionally crossing the road at a gallop. Grizzly sightings are always precious. They are much rarer in numbers in Yellowstone than bison, more reclusive, less tolerant of people, less likely to come out from behind the tall trees of the forest or frequent the road where they bump into people.

Bear jams occur because the big guys generate significant buzz. A park visitor may become jaded over bison sightings after viewing fifty, or a whole herd. No one tires of bear sightings. The top-of-the-food-chain animal is large and powerful, and everyone knows the bear's reputation as a potential man-killer.

People still tend to take risks to click a camera and make a souvenir. Unless they are hiking in the backcountry or at a remote campsite and a bear wishes to check them out, most bears in Yellowstone seen by tourists are a safe distance off. Most.

Once a bear is spotted and lingers in an area, word spreads, cars pull over to the side of the road, not necessarily legally or intelligently parked, riders leap out and run toward the bear to shoot those photographs. Sometimes the bear is oblivious, comfortable on a perch behind some downed timber on a hill, demonstrating no interest whatsoever in clambering down in the direction of the commotion. This is especially true if the bear has found goodies to munch on. He couldn't care less if people take his picture from a distance, as long as they are not in his path or interfering with his food source.

I have spent up to half an hour firing off picture after picture, watching a bear eat, watching a bear investigate another patch of grass, watching for that moment when he lifts his big, round, amazingly large head while pausing for breath instead of gobbling more and more calories down his throat.

Typically, one by one, drivers left, as if the drivers' and passengers' own appetites had been sated by this bear sighting. Rangers arrived to control traffic, but no one tried to shoo me away. Newcomers drove up and desperately sought an opening for their car, or even just a moment to gain a good angle by leaning out a window and shooting pictures on the move.

Sometimes the opportunity was so bountiful people did weary and, keeping to some schedule, simply drove off while the picture-taking was still good. I don't ever recall being the first on the scene with a bear to instigate my own bear jam. But sometimes I outlasted everyone else who had been there before me, only to be replaced by fresh faces.

Once, I pulled into a bear jam that was blocking traffic on both sides of the road. There were two bears on a plateau, almost too far away to obtain a single good photograph before they ambled away. I had been to the area before and tried to think like a bear. I speculated the mother and cub might cut through the woods and come out on the other side on a curve of the road.

I drove ahead and I was right. They broke out of the woods right in front of me. I was the lead driver, and they crossed the street between my car and the oncoming halted line of traffic. While I congratulated myself for this maneuver, the bears took one look at all of the cars and hustled across the road, ducking into a fresh stand of trees and disappearing.

A similar event occurred when I drove down the road guessing where I thought bears might emerge from the trees. They did so, and soon there was a whole bunch of people gazing at them from one hundred yards away. Only the bears did not stay on their originally chosen path. They began doubling back, heading straight for the people. As individuals retreated to cars for protection, the duo kept on coming, crossed the road and, rather remarkably, set up right there, finding the pickings edible.

Whole groups of people followed on foot while attempting to maintain distance. The bears stuck around for some time. They moved parallel to the road, eating as they went. When I at last had clicked my fill, I began retreating back to my car, leaving the bears and their fans together some fifty yards to my rear. I realized I had kept walking farther and farther from my car.

Unexpectedly, the bears changed direction. They retreated back along the side of the road, out of sight, leaving behind the visitors, and then suddenly rose over the lip of the road to cross back to the other side, no more than ten yards from me. I froze, caught in the open, as the bears dashed across the street back into the trees. I was fortunate they didn't run me over. There was nothing I could have done if they came at me, even accidentally, not maliciously. I was wide-eyed and recognized I had experienced a close call. Since most of the people were up the road, there were hardly any witnesses. But a moment later a man in a pickup truck pulled up next to me and asked if I was that guy who had almost been bowled over by the bears.

I have never seen a bear in Yellowstone winter. I assume they were always hibernating. Over the years I have taken snowcoach tours from more than one direction and once got a break on a winter visit when it was so warm I was able to drive my own car on snow-free roads out of Mammoth Hot Springs to the Lamar Valley.

Winter in Yellowstone intrigued me enough I signed up for a snowmobile tour. I had zero experience driving a snowmobile, though I kept being told how easy it was to steer when traveling at up to thirty-five miles per hour.

I was with a small group of strangers and a guide. Helmets and complete snowmobile suits were provided, but I was still convinced at some point I would be freezing. Wrong. The equipment was more than adequate, even though the

Old Faithful lets loose with its powerful eruption of steam.

wind roared periodically and we even got snowed on at different times.

The park seemed almost empty without cars, with few snowcoaches overlapping. Everything about the park looked different under snow than in summer when the whole region consisted of brown mountains and green trees and grass. It was a worthwhile journey—though tiring—and problems I encountered were attributable to operator error. Me.

The lowlight was when I skidded the snowmobile slightly off the side of the road, just a foot or two, but got stuck in a snowbank. I turned the engine off and on and as I stepped on the gas to roar back onto the road it stalled and in almost slow motion tipped over. One leg was pinned to the ground. It looked worse than it was. I was not actually hurt because the cushion of the snow prevented any violence being done to my body. The problem was I could not gain purchase in the deep snow to obtain a good enough grip to move the machine off me. I was stuck. It took help from two other men to lift the machine right side up.

Everyone was very solicitous, wondering if I was harmed. Only my ego. It was embarrassing. It was somewhat like skidding slightly off the road in your car at fifteen miles per hour and crashing into a plastic garbage can. Everything about the "accident" looked pathetic, but neither metal nor bones were broken nor scratched.

I have been a man for all seasons in Yellowstone and enjoyed them all, though sometimes strong sunshine diminishes the experience because it sends animals scurrying for midday naps and you can drive and drive and not see wildlife because of the siestas.

Many regular visitors speak in favor of visiting the park in early morning, just after sunrise, when animals begin to stir from overnight slumber, on the prowl for breakfast. I am not a morning guy, so those with the commitment to visit Yellowstone at 5:00 a.m. usually are not going to come across me.

The more time overall spent inside the park, the better the odds of coming across wildlife. The more time invested, the more you see. As someone who lived adjacent to the park I never spent the night in park hotels, even if my driving day ended in the dark when I could no longer see scenery or animals.

Autumn always seemed special. October brought fall foliage, wildlife stocking up on winter stores. There were always fewer busloads of tourists or carloads of families, so it was easier to move around. Planning for lunch, or even a restroom, was required because one by one the general stores closed as the end of the season approached.

Once, I came across two elk duking it out, antlers to antlers in battle, at the travertine terraces at Mammoth Hot Springs. The fight was probably over a female since it was the rutting season, but her ladyship was not in view. This battle went on for some time, though with pauses and periodic backing off. The elk were still at it when I left the scene, unsure which animal had the upper hand. Being present for elk tangling

was a one-time occurrence. It was a reminder what a privilege it is to see wildlife in wild habitat, living lives on their own terms, ignoring the people checking them out.

It is never a sure thing gambling on animal behavior except wolves being in short supply. Black bears don't seem to have the same cachet as grizzly bears, but many black bears are big for their age and can be just as dangerous. One summer a black bear invaded a campground and bit a woman on the thigh through the wall of her tent. That same year a particularly reckless black bear invaded a campground and actually beat on automobiles.

The big dude I encountered at the road junction near Tower and Roosevelt was tamer. That black bear focused more on ingesting grassy plants and staying clear of mischief. Still another black bear discovered ten pounds of people food left carelessly unprotected on the Lamar River Trail. When rangers tried to scare the bear away it

This full-grown ram is relaxing on a warm afternoon.

refused to budge, feeling it had squatter's rights. This was an unsuccessful strategy and park personnel euthanized it.

You never know what wildlife scene or incident or animal you will come across, whether you will gaze upon your fill of bison, elk standing in a river, sheep reclining by the side of the road, a wolf miscalculating enough to show itself, or a grizzly bear, the king of this jungle.

In 2022, celebrating the one hundred fiftieth anniversary of its founding, Yellowstone was branching out, in some cases honoring its historical roots with Native Americans and in other ways with educational offerings. Reminding visitors of the eleven thousand years of Native American connection to the region, the millions who visit the Old Faithful area were to be exposed to a Yellowstone Tribal Heritage Center project. A large tribal tepee village was to be erected at the Roosevelt Arch, too. Taking note of the passage of the years since Ulysses S. Grant affixed his signature to the original enabling legislation, the University of Wyoming scheduled a 150th Anniversary of Yellowstone Symposium. Taking stock of the time gone by, assessing the changes and the sameness of Yellowstone, it figured to be a year of reflection. The year-long birthday party highlighted Yellowstone's foundational attributes.

Yellowstone National Park is always a lure, always a treat, always inviting regardless of the season, in the coolness of autumn, the cold of winter [rearranged for chronological order], the sparkling growth of spring, or what sometimes seems to be the madness of summer. It is always a beauty, and its beasts are part of its attraction.

The Yellowstone fan club membership is filled with lifers who never tire of visiting and drinking in the offerings of the nation's first national park, who understand Yellowstone is a special symbol of America, set aside for its uniqueness.

About the Author

Lew Freedman is a prize-winning journalist and the author of more than one hundred books. He resides in Indiana with his wife, Debra, and dog, Boston. He previously lived in Cody, Wyoming, on the outskirts of Yellowstone National Park. His author website is www.lewfreedman.weebly.com.

Author Lew Freedman loves fishing for cutthroat trout on Yellowstone Lake.

The Park Service estimates that approximately 500 bighorn sheep inhabit the park.

Sources

Newspapers

Bozeman Chronicle (Montana)
Chicago Tribune
Cody Enterprise (Wyoming)
Idaho Statesman

Magazines

National Geographic, August 8, 2018.
Outing: Sport, Adventure, Travel, Fiction, May 2, 1897.

Books

Albright, Horace, and Frank J. Taylor. *Oh, Ranger!* Riverside, CT: Chatham Press, 1928/1972.

Black, George. *Empire of Shadows: The Epic Story of Yellowstone*. New York: St. Martin's Griffin, 2012.

Clayton, John. *Wonderlandscape*. New York: Pegasus Books, 2017.

Duncan, Dayton and Ken Burns. *The National Parks: America's Best Idea*. New York: Alfred A. Knopf, 2009.

Everts, Truman. *Lost in the Yellowstone*. Salt Lake City: University of Utah Press, 2015.

Haines, Aubrey L. *Yellowstone National Park: Its Exploration and Establishment*. Washington, DC: US Department of the Interior, 1974.

Hansen, Heather. *Prophets and Moguls, Rangers and Rogues, Bison and Bears*. Seattle: Mountaineers Books, 2015.

Lewis, Meriwether and William Clark. *The Journals of Lewis and Clark*. New York: Signet Classics, 2011.

Mernin, Jerry. *Yellowstone Ranger*. Helena, MT: Riverbend Publishing, 2016.

Miller, Mark M. *Adventures in Yellowstone: Early Travelers Tell Their Tales*. Guilford, CT: TwoDot, 2009.

Miller, Mark M. *The Stories of Yellowstone: Adventure Tales from the World's First National Park*. Guilford, CT: TwoDot, 2014.

Stark, Mike. *Wrecked in Yellowstone*. Helena, MT: Riverbend Publishing, 2016.